ASPECTS OF RURAL SETTLEMENTS AND RURAL SOCIETY IN EARLY MEDIEVAL INDIA

Sakharam Ganesh Deuskar Lectures on Indian History and Culture, 1985

Aspects of Rural Settlements and Rural Society in Early Medieval India

BRAJADULAL CHATTOPADHYAYA

PRIMUS BOOKS

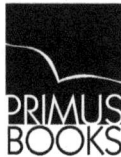

PRIMUS BOOKS
An imprint of Ratna Sagar P. Ltd.
Virat Bhavan
Mukherjee Nagar Commercial Complex
Delhi 110 009

Offices at CHENNAI LUCKNOW
AGRA AHMEDABAD BENGALURU COIMBATORE DEHRADUN GUWAHATI
HYDERABAD JAIPUR JALANDHAR KANPUR KOCHI KOLKATA MADURAI
MUMBAI PATNA RANCHI VARANASI

First published 1990
Reprinted 2017

ISBN: 978-93-86552-04-4 (hardback)
ISBN: 978-93-86552-35-8 (POD)
ISBN: 978-93-86552-05-1 (paperback)
ISBN: 978-93-86552-06-8 (e-book)

Published by Primus Books

Lasertypeset by Sai Graphic Design
Arakashan Road, Paharganj, New Delhi 110 055

Printed and bound in India by Replika Press Pvt. Ltd.

For

ARCHANA

and

BUBA

Contents

Preface to the Reprint

It is not customary to write a new Preface when a particular work is reprinted without any major modification or addition. The present work however, I feel, needs one. The original edition was published, on behalf of the Centre for Studies in Social Sciences, Calcutta, by K.P. Bagchi & Company, Calcutta in 1990. Its origin was in two lectures, delivered as Sakharam Ganesh Deuskar Lectures, 1985, on invitation from the Centre, in 1987. The lectures were enlarged for publication and an additional essay, apart from an Introduction and a Conclusion, was added to them. Since their publication as a book with the present title in 1990, much new material, particularly material pertaining to Chapter 2, and new commentaries have been published. The publication was followed by a long and important review article by V.M. Jha: 'Settlement, Society and Polity in Early Medieval Rural India', which appeared in *The Indian Historical Review*, vol. 29, nos. 1–2, 1993–4. In terms of source material, more important is the addition of newly discovered set of inscriptions bearing on the rural history of Bengal which is the theme of the second chapter of this book. Ably edited and translated with notes by G. Bhattacharya and, in greater number, by Dr. R. Furui of Tokyo University, the documents add substantially to what we know from previously available records. Dr Furui has also meaningfully analysed all available data in his unpublished Ph.D. thesis: 'Rural Society and Social Networks in Early Bengal from the Fifth to the Thirteenth Century', Centre for Historical Studies, Jawaharlal Nehru University, New Delhi, 2007. Dr Furui also came out wih a number of essays in different journals broadly bearing on the theme. I mention these because, before bringing out a reprint of a book first published in 1990, it was expected—and it was my expectation too—that I would appropriately update it and perhaps modify it, if required. My apologetic excuse for not doing so is that between 1990 and now my concerns have drifted away in other directions, not all necessarily academic, and I have not felt upto handling the arduous task of revising an already published work. More importantly, perusal through the new published documents has convinced me that even if I had undertaken the task of revision, it would have simply entailed the addition of some new material and not any major change in my approach to the material. My position now would have remained identical to what it was in 1990.

I am sincerely thankful to both the Director and Professor Rosinka Chaudhuri of the Centre for Studies in Social Sciences, Calcutta, for readily giving me required permission to get it reprinted.

Uttarpara BRAJADULAL CHATTOPADHYAYA

One

Introduction

EARLY MEDIEVAL India did not have a Montaillou, or rather, even if it had one, there is no way we can know about it. A document of the kind of the Fournier Register, on the basis of which Emmanuel le Roy Ladurie reconstructed the fascinating profile of a peripheral village society in medieval France,[1] is simply unavailable for a researcher working on early medieval India. It is only perhaps towards the end of the medieval period of Indian history that documents which were concerned with certain details of rural life and which may be organized into a somewhat regular series became available for some regions.[2] And yet, considering India's long-term agrarian history, rural settlements, in different geographical settings and of different sizes and structures, were the primary units in which human activities were socially organized. Since in these lectures I shall be concerned mainly with problems associated with studies of such units, I must first of all define the scope of my enquiry. I would like to do so by referring to sources and to historiography interminglingly.

The fact that our understanding of early medieval—or for that matter early historical—rural settlements and rural society is at the moment rather inadequate[3], may in a large measure be attributed to the nature of the sources available for these periods. My reference to the Fournier Register was only incidental; it is nevertheless true that we do not have any category of records for the early medieval period which may be used to focus on different dimensions of individual rural settlements or to reconstruct, satisfactorily, long-span chronological history. I would, however, hesitate to attribute the current state of rural historiography to limitations of sources alone. Even though attempts to prepare chronological history of village settlements and village communities in a regional context were made as early as 1927,[4] the trend has generally been to focus on themes like social and economic history, works on which generally incorporate—and rarely analyse—material relating to rural economy and society. Even in studies specifically devoted to the early medieval village—and there are not many of this *genre*—the profile of a village or of groups of villages as spatial human settlements, with particular forms of social organization, does not emerge in clear contours.[5] In the absence of micro-level studies, with the village as their main focus, such problems as the structure of relationship at the level of the rural society or relationship between rural society and systems beyond it have been more or less subsumed by generalities on 'agrarian system', 'agrarian structure', 'ownership of land', 'agricultural production', 'agrarian relations' and so on.

What general impressions we gather from historical writings and sources regarding early medieval villages are, however, exciting, and should encourage us to probe further. One of the impressions which the sources, not all necessarily of the early medieval period, provide is that space was differentiated and perceived as corresponding to different social spheres. The sphere where accepted societal norms could be prevalent was a *janapada,* and from the time of the Buddha, the three distinct types of settlements which constituted the *janapada* were *grāma, nigama* and *nagara.*[6] This, of course, was not a simple schema, universally applicable, and *grāma, nigama* and *nagara* certainly do not exhaust the early settlement terminology.[7] In the early medieval period, new terms and new distinctions arose,[8] but the essentials of the schema which conceived of a *janapada* as constituted by different types of settlements—rural and non-rural—continued. *Araṇya,* the forest, was in sharp contrast to a *janapada. Araṇya* was not a non-living space; it was also not simply a recluse for the hermits, although the stereotype of the hermit-forest equation continues in early medieval literature.[9] *Araṇya* incorporated *pallī*—a term which, despite its different usages, was employed broadly in the sense of a tribal village. I am wary of using the term tribal, and I am simply using it to suggest a contrast with a more complex society represented by a *janapada.* The equation between *pallī* and tribal village may be established by examining references, however incidental, to villages of the Śabaras, the Pulindas, the Niṣādas, the Bhillas and the Ābhīras—perceived as settlement units different from peasant villages in early medieval literature and epigraphy.[10] *Pallī,* however, was not invariably a tribal settlement; when it occurred in the context of a peasant village, it could mean a 'hamlet', an extension usually of an existing village.[11] The varying meanings of *pallī* or *pallikā* would, thus, be understandable only by examining the context in which the terms occur. Of much greater frequency were references to *grāma* and *pattana, pura* and *nagara*—the country and the town as it were, but one should be cautious about using readymade labels.[12] *Grāma* can be taken in the sense of a peasant village and since the focus of what I have to say in these lectures will be on *grāma,* certain further clarifications both about *grāma* and other settlement terms seem necessary. *Pallī, grāma* and *pattana* (or *pura* and *nagara*) as representing different types of settlements were not necessarily immutable categories. Internal changes as well as encroachments into tribal habitats having been continuous historical processes, *pallīs* could, over time, change into *grāmas.* There are indeed various early medieval epigraphic references to inroads into habitats of tribal groups; often such penetrations into tribal areas took the form of colonization, resulting in the transformation of a tribal/pastoral area into a nucleus of petty monarchical power and of new types of settlements. This process is excellently illustrated by changes in the names of places—say, from Bhillamāla to Śrīmala[13]—or by actual evidence of transformation of a tribal, or, let us say, non-peasant region. A set of inscriptions of the ninth century from Ghatiyala near Jodhpur,[14] which I have used on earlier occasions,[15] may be cited here for their very interesting and relevant details. Written around 860, these inscriptions speak of a village Rohinsakūpaka which was previously protectionless and, unfit for habitation by good people since it was 'infested by the Ābhīras'. Kakkuka, belonging to a segment of the Pratihāra lineage, constructed at Rohinsakūpaka *haṭṭa* decorated with 'variegated streets, went to the houses of brāhmaṇas, kṣatriyas (*prakṛti*) and vaiśyas, and promising them means of livelihood, established the *mahājanas* there'. Kakkuka's contribution to the rural landscape around Rohinsakūpaka seems to have taken the form of creation of sugarcane fields and mango-groves. Evidence of the kind available in the Ghatiyala set of inscriptions is rather rare, but there is no need to suppose that it stands as an isolated case. There are innumerable names of *grāma* in early medieval epigraphs, and contrary to the view generally held, many villages mentioned in connection with landgrants were old, settled villages. But transformation of non-peasant settlement regions into peasant settlement regions must have taken place also on a significant scale, proliferation of local-level polities perhaps contributing in a large measure to this transformation.

Grāma again, did not necessarily refer to a rigidly uniform kind of settlement, nor was it per se unchanging in character. A particular *grāma* could be a node in a cluster of rural settlements and could, thereby, illustrate the process of the formation of rural settlement hierarchy.[16] Even if one discounts the claim, often put forward in records from villages, that they were foremost among other villages,[17] some *grāmas,* owing to convergence of different historical factors, could indeed emerge as nodes in a cluster of rural settlements. Some *grāmas* could further develop into urban centres of some significance. The suffix *grāma* may have continued to denote a settlement space which had developed into an urban centre, but it was no longer a *grāma* in the sense of a village; it had passed into the category of an urban settlement, though retaining in some measure characteristics of rural space.[18] The process is further indicated by the change in the name of a place's suffix *grāma* to *pura* or *pattana*. *Nagara*, a generic term to denote urban centres could be a *pura*, a *pattana* or a *rājadhānī* or capital; distinctions, if any, between settlement characteristics of a *pura*, a *pattana* or a *nagara* are not very clear in the evidence available.

To return to the *grāma*, there are two major aspects of a *grāma*, as known from early medieval sources, which need to be discussed. The first aspect relates to *grāma* as an area of settlement. Although a *grāma* has sometimes been considered to be essentially a fiscal unit or an estate,[19] the point has been effectively controverted.[20] In fact, the manner in which *grāmas* are mentioned in epigraphic records would demarcate them as separate rural settlement units, distinguishable, in terms of their specified boundaries, from other *grāmas*. Even so, the physical components and spatial limits of a *grāma* could not always be self-evident. That there could at times be some confusion in the minds of early medieval men regarding what was meant by a *grāma* or what its spatial limits were, is interestingly illustrated in an alleged debate regarding the definition of a *grāma*, incorporated in an early medieval text *Abhidhānarājendra* of Vijayarājendra Surīśvara.[21]

According to this text, various opinions were put forward regarding the spatial limits of a *grāma*. One authority stated that *grāma* would include all that part of the land, up to which the cows of the village would graze; to this the pertinent objection was raised that the grazing area of cows could extend to what could be considered parts of other villages. According to another opinion, a *grāma* was stated as an area which the grass-cutters and wood-cutters covered in a day; to this view too objections were raised. A *grāma* was also viewed as an area served by a well, but this definition too was found unsatisfactory. In fact, the text does not resolve the problem of the definition of a *grāma*; it merely closes the debate by citing one authority which goes to the extent of suggesting that only a fenced or enclosed space corresponds to a *grāma*.

Despite the textual flexibility of its connotation—and this flexibility would perhaps derive to a large extent from the emergence of new *grāmas* and the possibility that *grāmas* could expand in space—the *grāma* (or its variants) was the essential reference point in the rural space of a *janapada*. If the boundaries of a *grāma* were not natural boundaries, they would be specified by referring to adjacent villages. Even when the spatial focus of a record was a large forest tract, which was in fact the object of a grant in the seventh-century Tippera inscription of Lokanātha,[22] the tract was defined by referring to villages bordering on it. As mentioned earlier, although *araṇya* (forest) and *janapada* with its rural settlements corresponded to two different kinds of space, the difference was by no means immutable, and the definition of a forest tract, infested with varieties of wild creatures, in terms of rural settlements bordering on it would be a pointer to the possibility of forest space transformation, in turn affecting the spatial arrangements of settled villages.[23]

But what were the constituent elements of a *grāma*? In studies of rural settlement patterns, structures of individual settlements and inter-settlement relationships are both important areas of investigation, but one may as well confess that material for such investigation is perhaps less than adequate in the sources of the period. Generally, a *grāma* was viewed as consisting of three components: *vāstu* (habitation), *kṣetra* (cultivated tract) and *gocara* (pasture).[24] The separation of *vāstu* from *kṣetra* would negate the unity of homestead and farmland, which should have important implications for an understanding of the organization of residential space in the village. There are, however, two problems here. First, it has yet to be examined how much the distinction drawn between *vāstu, kṣetra* and *gocara* was actually valid. It may have been so for many areas, but the blanket distinction would be injudicious to apply universally in view of the variations in rural settlement structures even within a single geographical region. Second, the epigraphic records which alone yield names of thousands of villages of the early medieval period are concerned either with the *kṣetra* component of a *grāma* or with the *grāma* as a whole; given their nature, they are not concerned with details of the settlement structure of a *grāma*. Further, details of the composition of the *kṣetra,* in terms of the distribution of cultivated plots or other features of the *kṣetra* area, do not necessarily occur in all records. Sometimes they do, and perhaps they are the only major key for obtaining a glimpse also into the social character of the *vāstu* component of a village.

This brings us to the second major point concerning the early medieval *grāma*. In terms of the composition of their social groups and of the pattern of authority within them, not all *grāmas* could be alike; but here again, it would be impossible to reconstruct a reasonably comprehensive range. From available historical writings a broad distinction can be made between *brahmadeya* and non-*brahmadeya* villages. This distinction extends, in the context of peninsular India, to two types of village organization: the *sabhā* which represented the village organization of a *brahmadeya* or an *agrahāra* or a *maṅgalam,* and the *ur* which represented a non-*brahmadeya* rural settlement.[25] In a way this broad distinction between *brahmadeya* and non-*brahmadeya* types of rural settlements is useful because it not only takes us away from the concept of an amorphous village community, but more relevantly, it should also immediately remind us of the fact that rural society as a whole cannot be analysed only with reference to the *brahmadeyas, agrahāras, maṅgalams* or *śāsanas* and to the privileges bestowed upon them by their patrons.[26] At the same time, there are certain risks also in assuming this distinction to be rigid. Apart from the fact that at any given point of time even an approximate ratio between *brahmadeya* and non-*brahmadeya* villages would be difficult to determine, even the suggestion that landownership in these two types of settlements was distinctly of two types, namely, communal in non-*brahmadeya* villages and private in *brahmadeyas,* remains *a priori* suspect.[27] Second, *brahmadeyas* were not necessarily *brahmadeyas* for eternity; there are instances where *brahmadeyas* resumed the shape of non-*brahmadeya* villages.[28] Far more frequent of course were cases of conversion of non-*brahmadeya* settlements into *agrahāras.* Although in all such cases of conversion political authority was involved, there is no way of knowing what contingent political or ideological imperatives prompted conversion of particular non-*brahmadeyas* into *brahmadeyas.* All that we know—and that too only in a few cases—is that such conversions could create tensions in rural areas to the extent of forcing royal power to ruthlessly suppress resistance.[29] But in the majority of cases it would be doubtful whether the creation of an *agrahāra* out of a non-agrahāra settlement would drastically alter the social composition of the settlement, whatever other changes it may have brought about.[30]

Another relevant dimension of rural historiography, which to some extent derives from the dichotomy between *brahmadeya* and non-*brahmadeya* types of villages, needs to be briefly touched upon. The stereotype of the self-sufficient village, in terms of its economy as well as its community structure, has often come under attack,[31] but has, curiously, been resurrected in the early medieval context in what may be called the Indian Feudalism formulation. The self-sufficiency of the early medieval village derives, in this formulation, from a concrete historical condition which is characterized, it is believed, by the absence of commercial exchange. The formulation, thus, envisages stages of change in rural settlements in economic terms which are thought of as being related to two major developments: (1) the self-sufficiency of rural settlements emerged because of the decline of exchange networks, implying that previously rural settlements in general were parts of such networks, and (2) rural settlements underwent further change through the process of being transferred to donees of various categories. The process and conditions of transfer undermined the communal structure of the village since the donees appropriated the rights previously communally owned, and in cases where the mobility of the social groups inhabiting the donated village was curbed, the self-sufficiency of the village was further reinforced.[32] In this formulation, thus, the village is essentially a closed entity, generating resources to the donee, and although prior to its transfer to the donee it may have been inhabited by different social groups, its image is that of an undifferentiated community with no movement from within toward social stratification or formation of inter-village networks.

The physical self-sufficiency of individual rural settlements has recently been questioned by referring to limited epigraphic evidence from early medieval Tamilnadu;[33] but even in approaches which are substantially different from the 'Indian Feudalism formulation'; the image of rural self-sufficiency or rural autonomy figures prominently. In these approaches, it is not villages as such which are seen to be autonomous; more important were supra-village but local level organizations, encompassing a group of villages. Here too the evidence is derived from inscriptions of early medieval Tamilnadu. In a detailed political geographical study of the *nāḍu* units with their component rural settlements in the Coḷamaṇḍalam during the Coḷa period, it was first argued that the *nāḍus* were not of the nature of administrative units but were basically local agrarian regions.[34] The point has now been stretched to the point of suggesting that there was an essential dichotomy between state power and rural community organization at *nāḍu* levels, and consequently, any effort by the state to penetrate local levels created situations of resistance.[35] This formulation appears somewhat curious when viewed in the light of suggested brāhmaṇa-peasant alliance in the formation of the complex of agrarian social organization of Pallava and Coḷa times.[36] Brāhmaṇa-dominated settlements, created by state power in fertile agrarian tracts, were as much a part of the *nāḍu* units as were settlements dominated by peasants.[37] To consider the *nāḍu* as originally a totally autonomous unit is perhaps not simply a reiteration of the image of closed village communities on an expanded scale; it adds to the problem of having to work out afresh the nature of relationship between the state and the productive units within its territorial expanse. In a recent critique of the notion of Brāhmaṇa-peasant nexus, the essential dichotomy, in early medieval India, between the interests of the Brāhmaṇas and those of the peasants has been vigorously stressed.[38] This is in line with the argument repeatedly advanced by the advocates of the Indian Feudalism formulation that creation of special rights by the state for the brāhmaṇas, as also in grants for secular service, was antithetical to communal rights. The mechanism of change in early medieval rural society is, thus, seen to consist in the undermining of 'peasant units' of production,[39] the agglomeration of which would perhaps constitute a definition of communal rights within a rural settlement. Polarization in rural society is, broadly speaking, represented by Brāhmaṇa-peasant dichotomy—a dichotomy created from above.

I have pointed out that rural settlements and rural society are not specific themes on which research is generally conducted, generalizations available about them in current historical writings being, thus, of a somewhat superficial nature. Generalizations on early medieval social trends vary substantially corresponding to the analytical approach adopted: there is, thus, the idea of 'Brāhmaṇa-peasant' polarity as opposed to the idea of 'Brāhmaṇa-peasant alliance' available for the same period of Indian history. However, the image of the rural society, as it can be constructed from these diametrically opposite views, seems to share certain common features. Rural settlements, either individually or at the level of a supra-village organization, initially stand at a distance from political power; political power intervenes, either for making grants or for enlarging its revenue base, and this creates change and situations of tension. The tension may be between political power and the autonomously organized agrarian units, or between state 'agents' such as brāhmaṇa landholders, temples or secular assignees and the original rural social groups. This view of rural society, I have suggested above, seems to ignore not only the differences among social groups in the majority of rural settlements but also other possible areas of tension within rural society: between brāhmaṇas, between brāhmaṇas and temples and within the ranks of secular landholders.

Having briefly introduced a few points which sources and rural historiography of the early medieval period raise, I must confess at this stage that the three case studies which together constitute the theme of my essays are inadequate for offering generalizations which would apply to early medieval rural settlements on a pan-Indian scale. In fact, the objective of these empirical studies is not to offer generalizations as such at this stage but to make, on a limited scale, regional comparisons. The regions selected for the present case studies are Bengal, south-eastern Marwar in Rajasthan and south Karnataka. Clearly, the volume of material available varies greatly from one region to another; thus, while it is impossible to prepare the chronological history of an individual rural settlement in early medieval Bengal, it may be possible to do so for a region like south Karnataka. This means that the units selected for study will differ from one region to another, but since the final purpose of the regional comparison undertaken through these case studies is to try and understand certain features of early medieval rural settlements and society, and not to reconstruct detailed rural history, the disparity between the units may not be considered a major methodological flaw.

It is difficult to provide a clear *rationale* for the choice of the three regions, mentioned above, for the present undertaking. To an extent, availability of source material, though different in contents in the three regions, is one criterion. But, even without subscribing to any notion of ecological determinism, the choice has perhaps been prompted by a desire to examine, initially, how rural settlements in these three regions differed in their access to and utilization of water resources. Bengal may be taken to represent a region which could be designated, to use two old expressions, as both *nadīmātṛkā* (watered by river) and *devamātṛkā* (watered by rain),[40] and would, thus, offer a geographical profile vastly different from those of western Rajasthan and south Karnataka. Although south-eastern Marwar is not a part of the desert zone proper, it nevertheless displays features of a semi-arid zone with extremely low and highly fluctuating precipitation, whereas the part of south Karnataka which lies to the east of *mal-nāḍ* proper experiences much lower degree of precipitation than do its western and coastal areas. Geographical differences bear upon the shape of the rural landscape, and ultimately, thus, the choice of the regions for study is not totally arbitrary but is dependent on how geographical features correspond to the landmarks in the rural settlements as they are described in the sources. The sources do not describe the villages in any detail, but village landmarks figure in specifications of village boundaries or of plots of land in cultivated areas. We shall be referring to these landmarks in some detail later on, but briefly, the manner in which early medieval villages of Bengal have been mentioned in the epigraphs would indicate their proximity to such sources of surface water as rivers, channels and streams. In south Karnataka, tanks were one of the major landmarks of rural landscape, whereas in south-eastern Marwar, the frequency and the manner in which wells figure in the inscriptions would tempt one to consider them, if we recall the argument put forward by at least one authority in the *Abhidhānarājendra* of Vijayarājendra Surīśvara cited above, as the central points around which villages could be defined. By referring to rivers and streams in the case of Bengal, to tanks in the case of south Karnataka and to wells in south-eastern Marwar we are not trying to view the rural settlements primarily in terms of how agriculture was practised in these regions; these landmarks are being seriously considered here to underline how the records themselves seem to make distinctions between rural settlements of different regions— distinctions which can be utilized for any preliminary empirical enquiry. It is these suggestions embedded in the records which we have tried to decipher and which will perhaps justify our repeated references to certain types of detail in the inscriptions, generally neglected in reconstructions of the early medieval history of India.

NOTES

1. The reference is to Emmanuel le Roy Ladurie's *Montaillou: Cathars and Catholics in a French Village 1294-1324* (translated into English by Barbara Bray, Harmondsworth, 1978) which provides a fascinatingly detailed account of a medieval village in the Pyrenees, close to the frontier between France and Spain.
2. I refer here particularly to the kind of documents which are presently being used for reconstructing the late medieval history of Rajasthan. See for example Dilbagh Singh. 'Caste and the Structure of Village Society in Eastern Rajasthan During the Eighteenth Century', *The Indian Historical Review,* vol. 2, no. 2, 1976, pp. 299-311; also the same author's, 'Local and Land Revenue Administration of the State of Jaipur (*c.*1750-1800)', unpublished Ph.D. dissertation, Centre for Historical Studies, Jawaharlal Nehru University, 1975.
3. No detailed studies of individual or even groups of rural settlements of the early historical period seem to be available as yet. For a specimen of an attempt to provide certain generalizations regarding the structure of village communities in the early historical period see G.M. Bongard-Levin, 'Some Problems of the Social Structure of Ancient India', in *History and Society: Essays in Honour of Professor Niharranjan Ray*, ed. D.P. Chattopadhyaya, Calcutta, 1978, pp. 199-227.
4. A.S. Altekar, *A History of Village Communities in Western India*, Bombay, 1927.
5. See for example A.K. Choudhary, *Early medieval village in north-eastern India: AD 600-1200*, Calcutta, 1971.
6. For discussions on early settlement terminology and on patterns of

settlements based on such terminology see N. Wagle, *Society at the Time of the Buddha,* Bombay, 1966, Chapter 2 and, A. Ghosh, *The City in Early Historical India,* Simla, 1973, Chapter 3.

7. Varieties of other terms such as *ghoṣa, kharvaṭa, puṭabhedana* occur in early historical sources. For comments see Ghosh, The City in Early Historical India.
8. For early medieval rural settlement terminology found mostly in literary sources from the north see Choudhary, Early Medieval Village, Chapter 3.
9. The equation as a literary stereotype occurs in Gupta and post-Gupta classics. See for example Kālidāsa's *Kumāra-sambhavam,* III, 24-34; for a detailed description of the hermitage in the Vindhayan forests in which a talking parrot gets its training in sacred lores see Bāṇabhaṭṭa's *Kādambarī,* ed. M.D. Pant, Delhi, 1971, *pūrvabhāga;* also C.M. Ridding, *The Kadambari of Bana,* Royal Asiatic Society, London, 1895. For interpretation of *araṇya* in the context of ancient Indian king's 'special relationship with the jungle—a relationship that is clearly related to transcendent authority' see J.C. Heesterman, 'The conundrum of the king's authority', in *The Inner Conflict of Tradition: Essays in Indian Ritual, Kingship and Society,* The University of Chicago Press, 1985, pp. 108-27. At the same time, the perception of *araṇya* or forest as a category in the sphere of human habitat comes through in the same literary texts. See for example *Kādambarī;* M.D. Pant, op. cit., p. 25; Ridding, *The Kadambari of Bana,* pp. 18-19, 80-1; also, E.B. Cowell and F.W. Thomas, The *Harṣa-Carita of Bāṇa,* repr., Delhi, 1968, pp. 225ff.
10. Choudhary, *Early Medieval Village,* Chapter 3.
11. For formation of hamlets which were incorporated within the physical limits of the main village see Chapter 4. See also Choudhary, Early Medieval Village, p. 45ff.
12. B.D. Chattopadhyaya, 'Urban centres in early medieval India: an overview', in *Situating Indian History,* eds. Sabyasachi Bhattacharya and Romila Thapar, Oxford University Press, New Delhi, 1986, pp. 8-33.
13. K.C. Jain, *Ancient Cities and Towns of Rajasthan: A Study of Culture and Civilization,* Delhi, 1972, pp. 155-63.
14. Munshi Deviprasad, Ghatiyala Inscription of the Patihara Kakkuka', *Journal of the Royal Asiatic Society of Great Britain and Ireland,* 1895, pp. 513-21; D.R. Bhandarkar, 'Ghatiyala Inscriptions of Kakkuka: Samvat 918', *Epigraphia Indica* (hereafter *EI*), vol. 9, repr., Delhi, 1981, pp. 277-81.
15. See my following essays: 'Origin of the Rajputs: the Political, Economic and Social Processes in Early Medieval Rajasthan', *The Indian Historical Review,* vol. 3, no. 1, 1976, pp. 59-81; 'Markets and Merchants in early medieval Rajasthan', *Social Science Probings,* vol. 2, no. 4, 1985, pp. 413-40.
16. See discussions in the following chapters.
17. One may cite here the example of Siddhala, a village of Rāḍha, for which the claim was made that it was 'the foremost of all and the ornament

of the fortune goddess of Rāḍha', N.G. Majumdar, *Inscriptions of Bengal,* vol. 3, Rajshahi, 1929, p. 36.

18. See my paper, 'Urban centres in early medieval India: An overview'.
19. '. . . We shall not be far from the truth if we understand *grāma* to mean an estate, comprising cultivated and fallow lands as well as pasture, and including any buildings, wells, etc., existing thereon; the area, in fact; that constituted the territorial unit for the purpose of revenue assessment', Prannath, *A Study in the Economic Condition of Ancient India,* repr., Allahabad, 1980, p. 33.
20. P.V. Kane, *History of Dharmasastra* (Ancient and Medieval Religious and Civil Law), vol. 3, 2nd edn., Poona, 1973, p. 140 fn 182.
21. Cited in Choudhary, *Early Medieval Village,* pp. 68-9.
22. R.G. Basak, 'Tipperah Copper-Plate Grant of Lokanātha: the 44th year', *EI,* vol. 15, 1919, pp. 301-15.
23. The contrast comes through in a comparison of Bāṇa's Vindhyan forest settlements with his description of Śrīkaṇṭha *janapada.* See *Harṣa-Carita* (E.B. Cowell and F.W. Thomas, *Harṣa-Carita*), p. 79ff.
24. For detailed discussion see Choudhary, Early Medieval Village, Chapter 3.
25. See K.A. Nilakanta Sastri, The *Coḷas,* repr., 2nd edn., University of Madras, 1975, Chapter 18; K.R. Hall, *Trade and Statecraft in the age of Coḷas* Delhi, 1980, Chapter 2.
26. Generalizations on early medieval rural society to be found in studies on 'Indian Feudalism' are largely based on sources which relate to grant of land and to privileges given to the donees.
27. N. Karashima, 'Allur and Isanamaṅgalam: Two South Indian villages of Chola Times', in *South Indian History and Society (Studies from Inscriptions, AD 850-1800),* Oxford University Press, 1984, pp. 3-15. For a critique of Karashima's analysis of relevant inscriptions see R. Tirumalai, 'Allur and Isanamaṅgalam revisited', in *Svasti Śrī* (Dr. B.C. Chhabra Felicitation volume), ed. K.V. Ramesh et. al., Delhi, 1984, pp. 25-55.
28. M.S. Randhawa, *A History of Agriculture in India,* vol. I, Delhi, 1980, p. 462.
29. For evidence of such resistance or of conflict arising out of conversion of peasant settlements into *agrahāras,* see N. Vanamalai, 'Consolidation of Feudalism and Antifeudal struggles during Chola Imperialist rule', *Proceedings of the Second International Conference Seminar of Tamil Studies,. Madras,* 1968, vol. 2, Madras, 1970, pp. 239-43; D.N. Jha, 'Early Indian Feudalism: A Historiographical Critique', Presidential Address, Ancient India section, Indian History Congress, 40th Session, Waltair, 1979; R.N. Nandi, 'Growth of rural economy in early Feudal India', Presidential Address, Ancient India Section, Indian History Congress, 45th Session, Annamalai Nagar, 1984.
30. Infra, Chapter 4.
31. The concept of the Indian village as a self-sufficient isolate derives from writings widely disparate both in affiliation and in chronology. Without going into any detail of the history of the concept, it may simply be

pointed out that the meaning of 'village community' which represents a crucial dimension of the concept of 'self-sufficient village' has had a history of shifting focus. In the first phase, it stood primarily for a political society—a republic; in the second, it represented a body of co-owners of soil, while in the third, it came to symbolize traditional economy and polity. See L. Dumont, 'The 'village community' from Munro to Maine' in *Religion, Politics and History in India,* Paris: The Hague, 1970, p. 112 ff.

In historical writings the response has been mostly to Marx's formulation of Asiatic Mode of Production in which the unity of agriculture and crafts is the hallmark of village self-sufficiency. Again, the present context does not require detailed reference to the debate surrounding the applicability of Marx's formulation. What may be underlined however is that even the critiques of the formulation (for example, D. D. Kosambi, *An Introduction to the Study of Indian History,* Bombay, 1956, pp. 10-11) envisage a stage in early Indian society in which the village closely approximates Marx's 'self-sufficing communities' (cf. for example, use of such expressions as 'growth of virtually self-contained villages' and 'closed village economy' in Kosambi, op. cit., pp. 226, 281), Villages, and even towns, are more self-sufficient in R.S. Sharma, *Indian Feudalism: c.300-1200,* University of Calcutta, 1965, Chapter 3, particularly p. 127 ff.

32. See the writings of R.S. Sharma on Indian Feudalism ranging: from *Indian Feudalism: c.300-1200* to *Urban Decay in India,* Delhi, 1987.
33. N. Karashima, 'Village Communities: Myth or Reality', in *South Indian History and Society: Studies from Inscriptions, AD 860-1800,* pp. 40-55.
34. Y. Subbarayalu, *Political Geography of the Tamil Country,* Tamilnadu State Department of Archaeology, 1973, pp. 29-36.
35. This point has been stressed in K.R. Hall, *Trade and Statecraft.*
36. This was formulated by Burton Stein, 'Brahman and Peasant in Early South Indian History', *The Adyar Library Bulletin (Dr V. Raghavan Felicitation Volume),* vols. 31-2 (1967-8), pp. 229-69; also Stein, *Peasant State and Society in Medieval South India,* Oxford University Press, New Delhi, 1980, Chapter 2.
37. See my review of K.R. Hall, in *The Indian Historical Review,* vol. 10, nos. 1-2, 1984, pp. 186-9.
38. D.N. Jha, 'Relevance of "Peasant State and Society" to Pallava-Coḷa Times', *The Indian Historical Review,* vol. 8, nos. 1-2, 1981-2, pp. 74-94. Jha points to the growing stratification within the peasantry itself, but does not elaborate; the 'social cleavage' that he talks about is between the brāhmaṇas and the peasantry, ibid., p. 79. For the levels at which the brāhmaṇas and categories of landholders are found in association with each other, at the exclusion of other categories, see Chapter 2.
39. See R.S. Sharma, 'How Feudal was Indian Feudalism', *The Journal of Peasant Studies,* vol. 12, nos. 2-3, 1985, p. 30.
40. Chaudhary, *Early Medieval Village,* p. 113.

Two

Some Aspects of Rural Settlements and Rural Society in Gupta and Post-Gupta Bengal

FOR A DISCUSSION on rural settlements and rural society in early Bengal, in any detail, one must of necessity start with the Gupta period. The emergence of rural settlements in Bengal, of course, substantially predates the Gupta period, but epigraphic references to them do not. Gupta period records contain useful—although hardly complete—detail regarding land, rural settlements and rural society which need to be analysed in order to understand certain processes of change in subsequent periods. The discussion attempted here is not comprehensive, but will be concerned with only two aspects. The general geographical distribution pattern of the rural settlements in Bengal from the mid-Gupta period onward, mentioned in copper plate charters, drawn up to record details of procedures for the purchase of land and making land gifts, is too well known to be repeated here.[1] Beyond the distribution of early rural settlements and the expansion of their geographical horizon over time, two relevant points which have not been sufficiently discussed so far are: (1) the spatial characteristics of the rural settlements and their relationship with natural, particularly, water resources, and (2) possible changes in the compositional and functional aspects of rural social organization. It is with these two aspects of the rural settlements of Gupta and post-Gupta Bengal that this essay will be primarily concerned.

Admittedly, sources for examining such aspects of rural settlements and rural society are extremely inadequate, and it is necessary to start by pointing out the limitations they impose on the enquiry. For undertaking an analysis of the distribution pattern and spatial dimensions of rural settlements, perhaps the most revealing evidence would be provided by the archaeology of rural settlements, but although we have a substantial quantum of data now on the emergence and distribution pattern of protohistoric rural settlements,[2] no such data extend to the Gupta and post-Gupta periods. A not entirely satisfactory alternative is to be found in the evidence of the land-transfer documents; but apart from the fact that references to village settlements in these documents are not uniform either in terms of localities, subregions or regions of periods, the documents relate more to cultivated or cultivable space than to rural habitational areas. There is, however, one type of evidence, found in land grants of different regions; but nevertheless not usually utilized either for understanding the spatial relationship between one rural settlement unit and another, or the pattern of landholding. This evidence is available in the form of the specifications, given in the landgrant documents, of the boundaries (*maryādā* or *sīmā*) of the areas granted. The boundaries sometimes correspond to natural landmarks, sometimes they are cultivated plots held by individuals or by religious establishments and yet at other times they indicate where contiguous villages begin. The boundaries, as specified in land grants, thus, imply a limit imposed by man in the vast expanse of rural landscape, and the limit essentially connects the demarcated area to a human settlement. The field was an extension of the habitat within the framework of a socially demarcated settlement unit, and if the three major constituents of a rural settlement, namely *vāstu, kṣetra* and *gocara* made up an integrated entity, then the field boundaries may be expected to provide a partial view of a settlement complex corresponding to a *grāma,* marked off from another *grāma.* Limits chosen by man often coincided with limits imposed by nature, and a study of the criteria for such choices is important in as much as they point to the *raison d'etre* of settlement location and to differences in settlement patterns. Frequent references to rivers, rivulets or channels in the Bengal epigraphs to which we would be required to draw attention will relate to this point. However, since details of field boundaries are not available in all records, one may feel tempted to generalize on the basis of limited evidence—a procedure fraught with risk on various counts. The conclusions that may be arrived at therefore, ought, to be taken to relate to the period and spatial context of the evidence cited. An extension of this caution would be to consider possibilities of other patterns in other periods and other areas.

I

In our initial query with regard to the spatial dimensions of rural settlements in Gupta and post-Gupta times, we may begin by pointing to a somewhat curious incompatibility between the statements of the geographers and those of the historians. According to Spate and Learmonth, '. . . the settlement pattern of much of Bengal (especially the East) is distinctive in that the homestead, and not the compact village, is the unit'.[3] As a general statement, this seems to contrast sharply with the generalization made by a historian on the strength of the epigraphic evidence from early Bengal: '. . . as far as available evidence indicates, they [the villages] were of the nucleated, not of the single farm type. That is to say, the rural population lived in compact groups and not in widely scattered habitations'.[4] The same position is reiterated by Niharranjan Ray who, after examining several landgrant documents, came to the conclusion: '. . . the *kṣetrabhūmi* adjoins *kṣetrabhūmi*; *vāstubhūmi* adjoins *vāstubhūmi;* sometimes the village adjoins [another] village'.[5]

While it is difficult to accept *prima facie* the geographers' generalization,[6] it is necessary to probe into the empirical base of the historians' assertion further. Although information regarding the composition of the *vāstu* (inhabited) area of the village in early Bengal is almost completely absent in the epigraphs—unlike the information available in south Indian epigraphs—there is nevertheless some indication of the separation of the *vāstu* as a 'compact' habitat area from *khila* or *kṣetra,* the cultivable or the cultivated area. This impression may be formed by a meticulous study of the details, where such details are recorded, of the distribution of plots in the *kṣetra* areas. If within the territorial limits of a settlement area defined as a village were found plots belonging to a mixed group of holders and if these plots were found to be consistently located in a separate cluster, then one would perhaps be entitled to consider the village as representing a 'nucleated' type rather than a dispersed one. This method of determining the nature and structure of individual settlements may have its limitations, but it may then be further crosschecked by referring to other settlements in diverse chronological and spatial contexts.

Details of locations in which land transfers took place are generally not available in the early Gupta epigraphs from north Bengal; but even so, the information provided by a few records is suggestive. The Dhanaidaha record from the Rajshahi district, which is dated in the Gupta year 133 (AD 432–3)[7] and which is the earliest record so far available in Bengal, gives us a rough idea of the composition of the inhabitants of a village (the name of it is lost). In addition to incorporating the expression *prativeśi-kuṭumba* which came to be stereotyped (and which simply indicates the existence of a community of cultivators), the record mentions two categories of inhabitants of the village: the brāhmaṇas and the *mahattaras.* At least 18 individuals from these two categories represented the prominent families of the village. The impression the record provides is of mixed composition of population in average villages; it may further run counter to any assumption that the social organization of an average village would correspond to a separable unit of *vāstu* and *kṣetra,* i.e., combined homestead and farmstead of a single or extended family. The impression is further strengthened by the regularity with which the combination *brāhmaṇādin-grāmakūṭumbinaḥ,* i.e., 'the *kuṭumbins* of the village beginning with the brāhmaṇas' is found in the records of the period. Although such evidence can be produced in profusion, it has to be admitted that it cannot be used to reconstruct the pattern of the distribution of residential plots—and from that to reconstruct the spatial alignments of different social groups—in a village. The evidence, as available, is merely such as would point to the basic separation between a composite residential area from a composite area of cultivation within the defined limits of a village. Generally, when an area was transferred through a land-grant, it could be specified in any of the following terms: (1) cardinal directions in which it was located in relation to the village, (2) adjoining plots or local landmarks, (3) landmarks defining the territorial limits of the village itself, e.g. a moat or a river, (4) apparently recognizable but unspecified limits of another village. For example, 4 plots of land transferred through the Kalaikuri-Sultanpur grant of the Gupta year 120 (AD 440),[8] also discovered in Rajshahi district, were, thus, located:

> Of the nine *kulya-vāpas,* one was enclosed by an ancient moat, with the Vāta river on the north and the borders of Gulmagandhikā on the west; two *droṇavāpas* were in Gulmagandhikā in its east, to the west of its first pathway, and the remaining seven *kulyavāpas* and six *droṇavāpas* were in Tāpasapottaka and Dayitapottaka in the *prāvesya* of Hastiśīrṣa and in Citravātaṅgara in the *prāvesya* of Vibhītaka.

Clearly, the phraseology which characterises the details in the initial part of the grant retains a distinct identity of the village, as the space occupied by its inhabitants and as separate from the wider space in which the grant land was measured, at least theoretically, in terms of its sowing capacity. The villages, further, were not isolated; the term *prāvesya* has been taken to suggest that several villages were joined together for the purpose of fiscal assessment.[9] Thus, the villages Tāpasapottaka and Dayitapot-taka were linked with the village Hastiśīrṣa, and Citravātaṅgara with Vibhītaka. Moreover, all the villages came together on the occasion of the grant which the inscription records. It, therefore, seems unlikely that the villages mentioned in the Gupta records of north Bengal were dispersed either in terms of their internal settlement structure or in terms of how they related to one another, both spatially and socially.

The kind of evidence cited above, however, lacks in details regarding the *'kṣetra'* component of a village and it is only when we reach the close of the Gupta period in Bengal that such details begin to appear in landgrant records. In this respect, it will be rewarding to have a close look at the grant portion of the Gunaighar record of the Gupta year 188 (AD 507) which comes from the vicinity of Comilla in Bangladesh and to analyse the pattern of the distribution of newly created and old holdings mentioned in it. The Gunaighar inscription[10] speaks of the creation, through a copperplate charter (*tamrapaṭṭa*) of an *agrahāra* of eleven *khila-pāṭakas* in the village of Udaka.[11] The area of land transferred was made up of five separate segments.[12] The first segment, consisting of seven *pāṭakas and* nine *droṇavāpas* lay between the limits of the *agrahāra* of Guṇaka and the cultivated plot (*kṣetra*) of the carpenter (*vardhaki*) Viṣṇu in the east; fields belonging to the royal monastery (*rājavihāra-kṣetram*) and to an individual, Miduvilāla, in the south; fields belonging to three individuals in the west and fields belonging to several individuals and a tank belonging to an individual of the Doṣī community (a community of cloth merchants?)[13] to its north. The second segment, measuring twenty-eight *droṇavāpas,* similarly, had the following four boundaries: to the east, the village of Guṇikāgrahāra (Gunaighar, the findspot of the inscription); to the west, plot belonging to the individual Pakka-vilāla; to the south, plot belonging to the royal monastery (*rāja-vihāra*) and to the north, a plot belonging to an individual perhaps of the Vaidya caste. For the third segment, measuring twenty-three *droṇavāpas,* not all specified boundaries are intelligible, but what can be made out indicates that in this particular case, all the bordering plots belonged to individual holders. Similarly, the fourth segment, measuring thirty *droṇavāpas,* lay between the plot of Buddhaka in the east, the plot of Kālāka in the south, that of Sūrya in the west and that of Mahīpāla in the north. It is not necessary to proceed further with other details of the record, as we shall be required to return to it once again; but some of the points which emerge from the evidence already cited and which relate to the present discussion may be made at this stage. The creation of the *agrahāra* mentioned in the record took place within the confines of a well-settled village (i.e. Udaka) in which the distribution of cultivated plots, lying in close contiguity to one another, covered a wide social cross-section: from individual holders (many of them mentioned in terms of their castes) to temples and *vihāras*. If this evidence is taken to reconstruct the area of the village habitat, then the impression is likely to be that of a compact, nucleated settlement stretching into the area of cultivated and cultivable land which bordered on other villages and *agrahāras*. The rural settlements of the Gupta period, mostly located in north Bengal, but, as evidence from the later phase shows, extending toward the east, seem, thus, to have been compact villages occurring within clusters of similar villages. But, it may well be asked, can a village like Udakagrāma, of which the Gunaighar record of the Gupta year 188 provides details, be taken as a typical rural settlement either in the Gupta or the post-Gupta period? In fact, contrary to the impression generated by the statement of the historians cited earlier, evidence regarding field alignments in the *kṣetra* component of the village is rather sparse in Bengal, and reconstruction, entirely on the basis of such evidence, of the nature and structure of individual rural settlements, therefore, will remain a tenuous task. One evidence to illustrate the difficulty may be cited. The Vappaghosavata grant of Jayanāga,[14] issued in late sixth century and relating to south Murshidabad—Nadia area in Rāḍha, records a gift in the form of the village Vappaghoṣavāṭa which bordered on the north and the east on Gaṅginikā (identified with the river Jalangi,[15] but it could have been any minor river); on its west lay land belonging to the brāhmaṇas of Kutkuṭagrāma held on the strength of copperplate charter; the eastern boundary, apparently extending toward the south, continued as follows:

> Issuing thence and running along the western, boundary of Āmalapautika-grāma (the boundary) is the *sarṣapa-yānaka,* it is limited by the same (boundary) as far as Bhaṭṭa Unmīlanasvāmin's grant; from the south thereof, (the boundary) turning along further by the same boundary to the north, proceeds as far as the boundary of Bharaṇi-svāmin's grant, thence in a straight line enters the pond of Vakhaṭa-Sūmālikā on the boundary of Bhaṭṭa Unmīlanasvāmin's grant, and goes as far as the same boundary of the brāhmaṇas of Kutkuṭagrāma.[16]

To those who drafted the grant, it must have seemed rational to specify the boundaries of the gift village in this fashion since it involved referring to a familiar natural boundary (i.e. the river), landmarks on the cultivated space (the *sarṣapa-yānaka* and the pond) as well as villages which adjoined the gift village, but even with these details it is not possible to know what the total settlement configuration of Vappaghoṣavāṭagrāma and other villages mentioned was like. One can reconstruct the relative positions of the villages bordering on Vappaghoṣavāṭa, and the most that can be deduced is that perhaps here too, as in Udakagrāma of the Gunaighar record, cultivated fields bordered on one another to cover a stretch generally uninterrupted by habitations, and, thus, spatial distinction existed between *vāstu* and *kṣetra.* For example, if the habitation areas in both Vappaghoṣavāṭa grāma and in Āmalapautikagrāma stretched in a linear pattern along the Gaṅginikā or the river, then the fields can be located to the south and west respectively of these two villages. The possibility of the linear nucleation of habitation units at these two settlements cannot, therefore, be ruled out.

It would nevertheless be hazardous to claim that Gupta and post-Gupta rural settlements throughout Bengal were of a uniform type. The possibility of typological variations, derived not only from variations in terrains in which they were located but also from the fact that historical conditions for the emergence of rural settlements, differed over space and time. In the epigraphs, such possibility is suggested by the presence of at least two types of conditions: (1) association of an area with a particular community, which would perhaps imply a unity of *vāstu.* and *kṣetra,* forming a small settlement unit around such a community, (2) creation of a new settlement over a large tract of land for individuals of a community of brāhmaṇas, in a new area. This could point to the possibility that when an area was colonized for the purpose of creating a new human settlement, the process may have led to the formation of small units around the holdings of an individual family, and a rural settlement locality could in that case be made up by a conglomeration of such units. The settlement characteristics of such a settlement would then derive from its being newly created, and the nature of relations between social groups present in it was likely to be somewhat different from that in settlements which had evolved over a long period of time.

To illustrate the first possibility, the evidence of a group of records of the Candra dynasty from Mainamati may be cited. The Mainamati plates were found at Char Patra Mura on the Mainamati-Lalmai range near Comilla in Bangladesh, incidentally in the same region which yielded the Gunaighar record and in which nucleated settlements of the late Gupta period seem to have been located. The first epigraph, of year 6 of Laḍahacandra,[17] records a grant of 3 plots of which boundaries for 2 plots are specified. Not all the expressions used in the record are intelligible, but of significance are expressions like Vappasiṁha-*voraka-grāma,* Sūpakāra-*voraka*, Buddhanandi-*grāma*, Bāleśvara-Vardhaki-*voraka*, Karavattī-*voraka*, Mahadeva-*grāma* and so on. Similar expressions used in specifying boundaries of plots granted occur in the second record of Laḍahacandra of year 6, which mentions 4 plots; expressions which are of significance are Brāhmaṇadeva-*voraka*, Kaṁsāra-Kaddapolaka-*grāma* and Sura-*voraka-grāma*. In trying to examine the distribution of the plots of land granted, one is immediately struck by the fact that here too the areas were specified as bordering on one another. For example, the second plot of Laḍahacandra's first record, which measured 8 *pāṭakas,* 4¾ *droṇas,* 5 *yatis,* 3 *kākas* and 2 *bindus* and lay in Vappasiṁha-*voraka-grāma* attached to Dollavāyikā, had the following as its boundaries:

(1) In the east, the posts (*kīlaka*) planted in the western extremity of the land belonging to Sūpakāra-*voraka* and Buddhanandi-*grāma* in the western half of a tank; (2) in the south the northern demarcating border (*āli*) of a plot of land belonging to Baleśvara-vardhaki-*voraka*, and also the southern bank of Govind-Oñchama; (3) in the west, the eastern demarcating border of a plot of land belonging to Oḍa-godhānikā; the post planted on the demarcating border which is the southern boundary of a plot of land pertaining to the *godhānī* (*godhānikā*); and the demarcating borders which are the southern and eastern boundaries of a plot of land belonging to Ghaṇṭārava; and (4) in the north, the southern demarcating border of Jayalamba-*grāma*.[18]

At a casual glance, the evidence would appear to be similar to that furnished by the Gunaighar record; the crucial difference would seem to be that in the Mainamati plates entire settlements (*grāmas*), and not just plots of land were named after individuals, sometimes specified in terms of their community affiliation (examples: Buddhanandi-*grāma,* Jayalambha-*grāma*, Kaṁsāra Kaddapolaka-*grāma,* Bāleśvara-vardhaki-*voraka*), and what was essentially designated as a cultivated area was also the name of a *grāma*. Thus, the terms *voraka* and *voraka-grāma* are both used interchangeably. D.C. Sircar takes *voraka* to mean land fit for cultivation of *boro,*[19] a type of rice sown in low swampy ground or along the banks of a river.[20] The recurrence of the suffix *voraka* in villages named after individuals, thus, seems to suggest small, dispersed settlements adapted to a particular type of terrain and a form of cultivation. Such settlements would perhaps be cited, for administrative purposes, with reference to a larger settlement unit like Dollavāyikā, mentioned above. A parallel of this pattern may be located in the Faridpur region (Kotalipada *pargana*) where the thirteenth century Madanpada grant of Viśvarūpasena[21] refers to Vārāyipada-*grāma,* 'the habitation of the Barayi (betel-vine growers)'.[22] In this case too, the individual village settlement would seem to have been associated with a particular community, and, therefore, was of an internal structure different from settlements which had a more heterogeneous social composition.

Creation of new settlements, mainly for the purpose of providing space for communities of brāhmaṇas, was one way in which settlement-formation took place in early medieval India, and in the absence of relevant details, one cannot even satisfactorily guess what physical shapes such settlements would assume. The seventh-century Tippera plate of Lokanātha, from the Comilla region, provides one such example of the creation of a new settlement of a group of brāhmaṇas in what was obviously forest land (*aṭavi-bhūkhaṇḍa*), inhabited not by human beings but by wild animals (*mṛgamahiṣa-varāha-vyāghra-sarīsṛpādibhir-ryatheccham-anubhūya-mānagṛha-saṁbhoga-gahana-gulma-latāvitāne*).[23] Candra king Śrīcandra's Paschimbhag plates from Śrīhaṭṭa, written around 930,[24] recorded the creation of an immensely large settlement called Brahmapura-Candrapura over an extensive tract which covered three *viṣayas.* The new settlement was intended to accommodate not only six thousand brāhmaṇas who were given six thousand plots of land of equal size, but also had in it several temple-*maṭha* complexes and representatives from a number of other communities (for details see Appendix 4) who were settled on the Brahmapura to provide varieties of services to it. What kind of settlement structure was likely to have evolved at Brahmapura-Candrapura? One can only guess, but since the six thousand donees were given six thousand plots of land of equal size and these plots were further demarcated from lands given to various communities attached to temples, a few tentative suggestions may be made. The Brahmapura-Candrapura *śāsana* was too extensive to have evolved as an average village settlement, and it would seem unlikely that in the broad area in which six thousand brāhmaṇas were settled, there would have emerged a unity of residence and cultivation. Brahmapura-Candrapura, in other words, was unlikely to have developed into a single nucleated rural settlement; it was more likely to have developed into a rural settlement cluster, the social character of which would be defined by the domineering presence of a sizeable brāhmaṇa population.

Depending on the historical conditions of their emergence as also on the terrains in which they were located, it would seem then that the physical structures of rural settlements in early medieval Bengal were varied. This generalization is of course hardly adequate, but then the pieces of the jigsaw-puzzle which can be retrieved from the somewhat reticent inscriptions are hardly adequate either. Despite variations, there are, however, two characteristics which, if not universal, seem nevertheless to connect the Gupta and the post-Gupta rural settlements located in different subregion of Bengal. The first is that rural settlements, in the way they figure in the inscriptions, had close access to surface water in the forms of rivers, rivulets, channels and ponds. In fact, villages located between rivers and channels are often found to have had ponds (*puṣkariṇī*), sometimes privately owned, located in their *kṣetra* areas. In many cases, it is true, rivers or channels do not figure as natural boundaries, but then ponds do as landmarks for the cultivated area. While it is not possible to put together all relevant details from the epigraphs, a few samples may be chosen. Perhaps the most significant details in this regard, for the Gupta period, are those which occur in the Gunaighar record of AD 507 (see Appendix I). The boundary specifications of the five plots of land, which were the objects of the grant, mostly refer to adjoining plots and villages, but they also mention *Doṣī-bhoga-puṣkariṇī, Daṇḍa-puṣkariṇī* and *Gaṇeśvara-vilāla-puṣkariṇī* in addition to channels and streams for which several varieties of expressions such as *jola, khāta, Gaṁgā* have been used in the record.

At Gunaighar, plots belonging to individuals abound; the incidence of *puṣkariṇīs* belonging to individuals is also significant. At Egra, located in the largely different terrain of Midnapore, evidence regarding the distribution of plots or regarding the relationship of the settlement to any such natural landmark as a river is absent, but here too the 100 *droṇavāpas* of gift land in the village of Āmra-garttikā had several *puṣkariṇīs* as their boundary landmarks: *Tālapuṣkariṇī* to its south, *Vāhidakīya-sṛṣṭodaka-puṣkariṇi* to its west and *Caṇḍāla-puṣkariṇī* to its east.[25] The grant recorded in the seventh-century Tippera inscription of Lokanātha was that of an extensive forest-tract, but even here, the forest tract is mentioned as having bordered on *mahattara-Raṇaśubha-puṣkariṇi,* i.e. the tank of *mahattara Raṇaśubha.*[26] Construction of large tanks was sometimes a compulsion urged by the terrain; individual initiatives in this direction are highlighted in eulogies recording multifaceted achievements of the sponsors. The Bhuvaneswar *praśasti* (*c.* eleventh century) of Bhaṭṭa Bhavadeva records: 'In *Rāḍha,* in the waterless [*ajalāsu*] *boundary-lands* abutting on a village situated in an arid region, has been made (i.e. excavated) by him a reservoir of water (or tank) which gladdens the soul and mind of the company of tourists* sunk in fatigue. . . .'[27] [emphasis mine].

In general, however, the rural settlements which figure in the available epigraphic records are described as located in close proximity

* A more appropriate translation of the term would be 'travellers'.

to natural sources of surface water or to what were essentially extensions of such sources. An excellent document showing this correlation is the early ninth-century Khalimpur record of the Pāla king Dharmapāla,[28]—which, with its details of the boundaries of several villages given away in donation, may be cited as a sample:

1. The village (*grāma*) of Krauñcaśvabhra:

Western boundary	*Gaṅginikā* (small river)
Northern boundary	small temple (*devakulikā*) of Kādambarī and date-palm tree.
East-north boundary	*Āli* (*āl,* embankment?) constructed by *rājaputra* Devaṭa
East boundary	partly intelligible expression: *'Viṭakāliḥ Khātakakhānikāṁ gatvā praviṣṭā'*

The boundary specifications of the village Krauñcaśvabhra continue further from this point but many expressions used in the record are impossible to make out. The construction of an *āli* which constituted one limit of the village by *rājaputra* Devaṭa is significant. The parts of the boundry specifications which cannot be translated satisfactorily contain expressions like *Vilvārdha-strotikā,* and *Jambuyānika* which are taken to refer to other water courses.

2. The village of Māḍhāśālmalī

Northern boundary	Gaṅginikā
East boundary	Expression suggesting the existence of water course: *ardhasrotikayā āmrayānākolarddha-yānikaṁgata. . .*
South boundary	(village of) Kālikāśvabhra and water courses to the west extending to the Gaṅginikā (*Kālikāśvabhraḥ ato'pi niḥsṛtya Śrīphalabhiṣukaṁ yāvat paścimeṇa tato'pi Vilvaṅgorddhosrotikayā Gaṅginikām praviṣṭā*)

3. Pālitaka village

South boundary	Kāṇā dvīpikā (small island)
East boundary	Koṇṭhiyā *srotaḥ* (channel)
North boundary	Gaṅginikā
West boundary	Jenandāyikā (?)

These three villages included in the *Vyāghrataṭī-maṇḍala,* some times sought to be located in south Bengal, of Mahantāprakāśa *viṣaya.* The fourth gift village, Gopipalli, was, however, a part of Āmraṣaṇḍika-*maṇḍala* in Sthālikaṭṭa *viṣaya* and had the following boundaries:

East	The western boundary of Uḍragrāma-*maṇḍala*
South	*Jolakaḥ* (marshy land?)
West	*Khāṭikā* (ditch) named Vesānikā
North	*Go-mārga* (cattle-path) running on the borders of Uḍragrāma-*maṇḍala*.

It stands to reason then that colonization of new areas and creation of large scale settlements in them would be planned keeping in view their proximity to natural water courses. The Paschimbhag plates of the first half of the tenth century, to other details of which reference has been made in other parts of this essay, record the colonization of a large tract of land for a community of six thousand brāhmaṇas and several other social groups and for the construction of several temple—*maṭha* complexes. The settlement which was designed to cover an area comprising three localities (*tri-viṣaya*) was planned by the Candra king Śrī Candra, and with the exception of a boat-station (*naubandha*) the area of which was 52 *pāṭakas,* the total area taken up corresponded to previously unutilized space. In the broad design of the new settlement, called Candrapura-Brahmapura (*ityevaṁ Catussīmāparyantān Śrī Śrī Candrapurābhidhānaṁ Brahmapuraṁ parikalpya*),* the following were set to be the limits: on the east, *bṛhat-Koṭṭālisīmā* (*āli* or bank of earth thrown up to form a line of demarcation of the big fort?); on the south, Maṇi *nadī* (river); on the west, Jujju *khātaka* (channel), the Kāṣṭha-parṇī channel and the Vetraghaṭī river; and, on the north, the Kosiyāra river.[29]

Despite variations in boundary specifications—and the variations would be many, provided the relevant data in the inscriptions are discussed in detail—it seems that there was a recognizably consistent trend of regarding surface sources of water as landmarks isolating one rural settlement unit from another. This has important implications for trying to understand how a *grāma* was viewed as a *grāma* by those who surveyed gift lands, and the landmarks mentioned by them may be profitably compared, for this purpose, to those which figure in the villages of western Rajasthan and sourthern Karnataka which for the themes of the next essays.

* An alternative—and perhaps better—way to view it is to call it a 'Brahmin settlement named Candrapura'.

The second feature which seems to generally characterize the rural settlements and which, again, relates to the contemporary perception of rural space is that rural space, already developed as a *grāma* or even as yet undeveloped, was consistently defined in terms of other rural spaces, usually *grāmas* and at times other categories of inhabited space. This means that one inhabited space, a *grāma,* was an inhabited space in relation to another inhabited space; in other words, a settlement was essentially viewed in terms of spatial and social interaction, irrespective of whether there was nucleation or clustering of settlements or not. Thus, even before the *aṭavi-bhūkhaṇḍa* (forest tract) of the Tippera grant of Lokanātha was transformed into an area of settlement, the reference points for demarcating the area were the limits of two villages, Paṅga and Vāpikā, on one side and the tank of *mahattara* Raṇaśubha, obviously located in a settled village, on the other.[30] Whatever the distances between them, rural settlements were spoken of as relating to one another, and an area of settlement, despite its individual identity, was perceived as forming a part of an agglomeration. We close this section by referring to a record of the Sena period, a reading of which should provide an idea of the perception of rural space alignment. The Naihati plate of the time of Vallālasena, discovered in the Katwa subdivision of Burdwan district, records the donation of a village Vāllahiṭṭhā, located in Svalpadaksiṇavīthi of Uttara-Rāḍhāmaṇḍala in Vardhamānabhukti. The gift village consisted, according to the record, of certain specified measures of land, including dwelling places, canals and waste lands (*sa-vāstu-nāla-khilādibhiḥ);* its location is stated elaborately in terms, inter alia, of other gift settlements and natural boundaries in the following manner:

(1) To the north of the river Siṅgaṭiyā flowing to the north of the village [*śāsana* or village given in *śāsana*] of Khāṇḍayillā; to the northwest of the same Siṅgaṭiyā where it flows to the north of the village of Nāḍicā [*śāsana*]; (2) to the west of the same river Siṅgaṭiā where it flows to the west of the village of Ambayillā [*śāsana*]*;* (3) to the south of the southern boundary wall [*śīmāli*] of Kuḍumvamā [village], also of the boundary wall [*śīmāli*] going to the western direction on the west of Kuḍumvamā, of the cattlepath [*go-patha*] to the south of Auhāgaḍḍiyā [village] and of the boundary wall which commencing from the cattlepath to the north of Auhāgaḍḍiyā goes in a westerly direction to the northern boundary wall of Surakoṇagaḍḍiākīya (village); (4) to the east of the eastern boundary wall of the village [*śāsana*] and partly to the east of the cattlepath to the east of Jalasothi village [*śāsana*] as well as of the cattlepath up to the river Siṅgaṭiā to the east of the village [*śāsana*] of Molāḍandī.[31]

II

The spatial characteristics of rural settlements could, in many ways, be related to the manner in which rural communities were organized. Rural communities in pre-modern India have often been viewed as corresponding to basically self-sufficient units, but analyses of the nature of references to villages in epigraphs seem to produce the impression that a closed system would be incompatible with the way the rural settlements were spaced in relation to one another. Further, if the holdings of an individual or those of a religious establishment were spread over a number of villages—and this was the case in Puṇḍravardhana-*bhukti* in north Bengal when land for a Jaina *vihāra* was acquired at 4 villages[32]—then it would be entirely unlikely that the functional network of an individual or of those managing a religious establishment would remain limited to a village or a single defined settlement unit. Second, as will be elucidated later, on the basis of the

Map 2.1: Some villages mentioned in the Naihati plate of Vallalāsena

sixth century Mallasarul and other similar epigraphs, when there was close contiguity between *agrahāra* type settlements, important rural issues such as purchase or gift of land would draw them together and would be decided upon by representatives from various *agrahāras*. There was, moreover, always the possibility that rural settlements would be functionally integrated with administrative/political centres at local[33] as well as supra-local levels, and if the evidence for the mechanism of this integration is not always all that profuse, there is enough in the Puṇḍravardhana-*bhukti* inscriptions of the Gupta period to suggest such integration.

Finally, in a new settlement—for example, an *agrahāra* settlement or a settlement centring around monastic establishments—created by a political authority of whatever level, its internal structure would essentially relate to its *agrahāra*/monastic character, and, moreover, the nature of its relationship with other types of settlements would tend to be different from that between average rural settlements. This assumption could further extend to areas in which there was concentration of secular elites or of their landholdings. It would be difficult to locate such concentration as a consistent pattern, but where it does occur, it must have had significant bearing on the social structure of the rural settlement area concerned. Thus, the Sunderban plate of the time of Lakṣmaṇasena (twelfth century)[34] lists five contiguous plots of land (*śāsana*), in the village Kāntallapura *caturaka* (suggesting that the village headed a group of 4 villages) situated in the Khāḍi-maṇḍala (Diamond Harbour area) in Puṇḍravardhana-*bhukti*, held by *Śāntyāgārika* officials Prabhāsa, Rāmadeva, Viṣṇupāṇi Gaḍolī, Keśava Gaḍolī and Kṛṣṇadharadeva Śarman—suggesting a domineering presence of official elements in the affairs of Kāntallapura *caturaka*.

If rural settlements and rural communities were not isolated, they were not characteristically unchanging either. In this section, we shall endeavour to examine one dimension of change from the mid-Gupta through late Gupta to the immediately post-Gupta and early medieval periods by focusing on the 'community' organization at the village and supra-village levels. In such an endeavour, several components in the total structure of the inscriptions, and particularly those components that alter radically with the passage of time, need to be looked into closely. Changing phraseology, and of course the nature of the contents of the relevant components of the inscriptions, are important indicators of changing relationship between political authority and the village, and, therefore, of the internal organization of the village. Several mid-Gupta inscriptions from north Bengal refer to a body called *grāmāṣṭakulādhikaraṇa,* and in our attempt to understand the nature of community organization at the rural level at this stage, our initial focus would be on this body and its relationship with the Gupta state.

The *grāmāṣṭakulādhikaraṇa* is mentioned in the Gupta records in connection with land transactions and, therefore, references to it among a hierarchy of *adhikaraṇas* (offices) indicate the manner in which a particular functional level at the village figured on occasions which incorporated it with supra-village levels. Perhaps the earliest reference to *grāmāṣṭakulādhi-karaṇa* is found in the Dhanaidaha copper plate, from the Natore division of Rajshahi district, of the time of Kumāragupta I (Gupta year 113 = AD 432).[35] The record is very much damaged and, therefore, does not yield satisfactory details, but from what is preserved it appears that an *āyuktaka* official approached the *kuṭumbins,* the brāhmaṇas, the mahattaras and the *grāmāṣṭakulādhikaraṇa* since he desired to purchase one *kulyavāpa* of land by destroying the *nīvi-dharma* (the non-transferability of it). The land was being purchased for the purpose of making it into a grant for a Vaidic brāhmaṇa. Better details about *grāmāṣṭakulādhikaraṇa* appear in later records, but even from this damaged earliest reference two points seem to emerge: (1) the *grāmāṣṭakulādhikaraṇa* was not an all-comprehensive village body since different social groups in the village (*kuṭumbins,* brāhmaṇas, *mahattaras*) figure separately from the *adhikaraṇa.* The relative importance of the brāhmaṇas and the *mahattaras* is indicated by the fact that individuals belonging to these catagories are mentioned by name; (2) in a situation when land was alienated, consent at the rural level, involving various categories of rural people, was necessary. We shall see that such consent was necessary even toward the close of the sixth century but by then the social context of the consent had undergone radical changes.

The next reference to *grāmāṣṭakulādhikaraṇa* occurs in the Damodar-pur (Dinajpur district) copperplate of the time of Budhagupta (Gupta year 163 = AD 482–83).[36] It is stated in this record that when Nābhāka, a resident of the village Caṇḍagrāma, put in a request for the purchase of a plot of land, the *mahattaras,* the *aṣṭakulādhikaraṇa,* the *grāmika* and the *kuṭumbins* informed, from Palāśavṛndaka, the brāhmaṇas and other residents (*brāhmaṇā-dyānyakṣudraprakṛti-kuṭumbinaḥ*) of Caṇḍagrāma of this request, after enquiring into their welfare (*kuśalamuktvā-nudarśayanti*). Without going into details of the other parts of the transaction, it may simply be noted that when the plot of land was measured for the purpose of sale, it was so done by the '*mahattaras* and others, officers and householders' *mahattarādyādhikaraṇakuṭumbibhiḥ*). One further point emerging from the record is that *aṣṭakulādhikaraṇa* of Palāśavṛndaka alone did not communicate to different categories of residents of Caṇḍagrāma the request for the purchase of land; the *aṣṭakulādhikaraṇa* was associated in this task by the *mahattaras, grāmikas* and *kuṭumbins.* What is also pertinent is that the communication went from Palāśavṛndaka to Caṇḍagrāma and that Palāśavṛndaka had an *āṣṭakulādhikaraṇa* which apparently Caṇḍagrāma did not have. Since the land which was purchased bordered on Vāyigrāma (Baigram) which also has yielded a copper plate of the Gupta period, it may be useful to get this impression confirmed by referring to the inscription from Baigram. The Baigram record (Bogra district) is dated in the period of Kumāragupta I (Gupta year 128 = AD 447-48) and is thus earlier than the Damodarpur record of 482-3 just cited. Vāyigrāma of Baigram record[37] too did not have an *aṣṭakulādhikaraṇa*; in fact, Pañcanagarī, the *viṣaya* in which Vāyigrāma was located, also does not seem to have had the kind of full-fledged *viṣayādhikaraṇa* (district level office) which another *viṣaya,* Koṭivarṣa, had. It has been tentatively suggested that 'Koṭivarṣa . . . was perhaps a more important *viṣaya* where Government had to keep better administrative arrangement for the *viṣayādhikaraṇa* than in Pañcanagarī of this grant, which may have been a newly formed district at the time.'[38] As stated in the record, application for the purchase of land was made by two brothers, *Kuṭumbi* Bhoyila and *Kuṭumbi* Bhāskara who lived in the locality constituted by Trivṛta, Śrī Gohālī and Vāyigrāma (*Vāyigrāmika-Trivṛta-Śrīgohālyoḥ*). The communication regarding the application was in this case conveyed by *Kumārāmātya* Kulavṛddhi, head of Pañcanagarī *Viṣaya,* to the *viṣayadhikaraṇa* and to 'village householders, along with the brāhmaṇas and others and the Chief-officers (*saṁvyāvahārins*) of (the two localities named) Trivṛta, Śrīgohāli connected with the village named Vāyigrāma' (*Vāyigrāmika-Trivṛta-Śrīgohālyoḥ Brāhmaṇottarān Saṁvyāvahāri-pramukhān grāmakuṭumbinaḥ Kuśalamanuvarṇya bodhayati vijñāpayati*). This piece of information does not include a reference to the existence of an *āṣṭakulādhikaraṇa* in the locality at this stage; it seems to have come into existence by the time of the Damodarpur record of 482-83 in neighbouring Palāśavṛndaka and to have included in its network several villages of the locality.

Thus, *aṣṭakulādhikaraṇa,* which is interchangeable with *grāmāṣṭakulādhikaraṇa,* was not a body universally present in all villages at all points of time. In its literal sense, the term *aṣṭakulādhikaraṇa*[39] may suggest that 'it was originally a village organ composed of representatives of several families and . . . based on close blood relations',[40] but in several contexts in which it figures, it was essentially a link between upper tiers of local political organization and villages interconnected in its network. Standing above individual villages, it nevertheless operated at this level in association with representatives of different social groups from the rural society such as the *brāhmaṇas, mahattaras, grāmikas* and so on. For further elaboration on the nature of this representation, we have to turn to other records of the period.

Of the levels through which administrative procedures concerning sale of land had to move, it was the *viṣaya* which was normally the highest. The official seals of the landsale documents had usually the name of the *viṣayādhikaraṇa* from which they were issued.[41] The *viṣayādhikaraṇa* comprised, besides its official head, the *Kumārāmatya,* representatives from four non-agriculturist occupational groups: *Prathama-Kulika* ('the chief artisan'), *prathama-kāyastha* ('the chief scribe'), *Sārthavāha* ('the merchant') and *nagara-śreṣṭhi* ('the guild-president of the town'). It would appear that till the middle phase of the Gupta period, in areas like Koṭivarṣa, representatives from rural agricultural communities did not participate in deliberations at the *viṣaya* level, although procedures involving sale of rural land did not unilaterally descend from the level of the *viṣaya.* But there were other localities in which the *viṣayādhikaraṇa* was not present. The *adhikaraṇa* in such areas existed at the level of the *Vīthi* which brought about administrative integration of a number of villages within it, possibly by incorporating smaller units of several individual villages. For example, the Kalaikuri-Sultanpur record of Gupta year 120-21 (AD 440-1), from Rajshahi district,[42] refers to the *adhikaraṇa* of Śṛṅgavera*vīthi* located at Pūrṇakauśika and to the communication addressed to the *grāma-kuṭumbas* headed by brāhmaṇas at the villages Hastiśīrṣa, Vibhītaka, Gulmagandhikā, Dhānyapāṭalika and Saṁgohālī by the official of the *Vīthi* and its *adhikaraṇa.* In the Jagadishpur plate of Gupta year 128 (AD 447)[43] from the same locality, the communication by the same official *āyuktaka* Acyutadāsa was addressed to the chief (*pradhāna*) *kuṭumbins* headed by brāhmaṇas of the villages (*brāhmaṇādin-pradhāna-kuṭumbinaḥ*). Both description provide important information on categories of rural social groups associated with the functioning of the *Vīthi-adhikaraṇa.* There is nothing to suggest that representatives from these groups constituted the *adhikaraṇa* in the same way in which the *prathama-kulika,* the *prathama-kāyastha,* the *sārthavāha* and the *nagara-Śreṣṭhi* were members of the *viṣayādhikaraṇa* of Koṭivarṣa. The Kalaikuri-Sultanpur plate and the Jagadishpur plate simply state, after giving lengthy lists of representatives of rural residents: *Vayaṁca vijñāpitaḥ* (that is, 'we too have been informed'). However, the fact that personal names of these representatives figure, under appropriate categories, in the plates in association with the *Vīthi* official and the *adhikaraṇa* headed by him would suggest that they were active participants in transactions recorded in the plates. This supposition may be further supported by comparing the compositions of the representatives in the two plates (for details see Appendix 2).

The first three categories figuring in the Kalaikuri-Sultanpur record, which is earlier in date, were those of *Vīthi-kulika, Kāyastha* and *Pustapāla* (record-keeper). Whereas the only *Vīthi-kulika* mentioned is Bhīma, there are seven individuals in the category of *Kāyastha* and two in the category of *Pustapāla.* This offers significant variation from the composition of the *viṣayādhikaraṇa* in which only one member from each category was represented. Another variation is evident in the long lists of names under two categories: *Vīthi-mahattara* and *Kuṭumbi*—categories which are absent in records issued from the *Koṭi-varṣa Viṣayādhikaraṇa.* The Kalaikuri-Sultanpur inscription lists eight names under the category *Vīthi-mahattara* and seventy-six names under *Kuṭumbi.* In the Jagadishpur plate, issued in the same area about eight years later, the categories *Vīthi-Kulika, Kāyastha* and *Pustapāla* do not figure at all; besides, only four names figure in the *Vīthi-mahattara* category and twenty-eight in *Kuṭumbi.*

It has been necessary to cite the above details to show that significant variations existed in the nature of the participation of local communities in administrative operations in the Gupta empire. These variations were not necessarily local since they were present in the same locality at different points of time. Local community participation was no rigidly structured system interacting with the Gupta system of administration. A reconsideration of the meaning of this participation in order to show how its pattern changed in subsequent periods is, therefore, necessary.

The lowest unit in the system was obviously the *grāma* but not all villages were alike either in terms of their importance as settlements or in terms of their social organization. Individual *grāmas* were often grouped together with one *grāma* as the centre of the group, an arrangement which must have led to the formation of hierarchy among *grāmas:* Palāśavṛndaka of the Damodarpur record of 482-83[44] appears to have been such a *grāma* (the suffix *vṛndaka* suggests formation of a group); Pūrṇakauśika of *Śṛṅgavera-vīthi* of Kalaikuri-Sultanpur and Jagadishpur records[45] was another. There are several more examples of such *grāmas* from the Gupta period inscriptions of north Bengal. Another level in the hierarchy, the level of the *Vīthi*, may be envisaged. The existence of these levels, which should counter any impression that rural settlements were undifferentiated, is linked up with the problem as to how rural residents related to these levels. Obviously, not all residents of all villages, were participants in the rural administrative process. This can be easily established by showing that individuals mentioned by name in the records in connection with landsale are not necessarily mentioned in association with an *adhikaraṇa* either at the *Vīthi* or some other level. For example, Bhogila and Mahīdāsā, residents of Gulmagandhikā, included in Śṛṅgavera-*Vīthi*, do not figure either in the list of *vīthi-mahattaras* or in that of *kuṭumbis* in the Jagadishpur copperplate of AD 447. Second, and this may be the rationale for the formation of village hierarchy, administrative decisions like the sale of land located in a particular village, is communicated to it by a level higher than the village itself. In some cases, the level was constituted by *mahattaras, grāmikas, kuṭumbis* and *aṣṭakulādhikaraṇa*; it was from them, functioning at Palāśavṛndaka, that the communication proceeded to Caṇḍagrāma. In other cases, such communication would originate at the centre of the *Vīthi.*

It appears, therefore, that the structure of rural community in Gupta period Bengal will have to be considered both in terms of the degree of stratification which existed at the rural level and in terms of the linkage between rural settlements and rural community organizations on the one hand and the official organs of the Gupta state on the other. These points require some further elaboration. From expressions occurring in the records (cf. *Brāhmaṇādin-grāma-kuṭumbinaḥ,* Kalaikuri-Sultanpur record; *Brāhmaṇādin-pradhāna-kuṭumbinaḥ,* Jagadishpur record; *Brāhmaṇottarān-samvyavahāri-pramukhān-grāmakuṭumbinaḥ,* Baigram record) it would appear that even in the early Gupta period, the brāhmaṇas were already a major landholding group in north Bengal, and this is further confirmed by the names[46] of individual brāhmaṇas who figure either as *kuṭumbis* or *mahattaras* associated with *adhikaraṇa* at the *vīthi* level (Kalaikuri-Sultanpur and Jagadishpur records). As among other landholders, there were two groups among the brāhmaṇas, one corresponding to the category of *kuṭumbis* and the other, to that of *mahattaras.* The fact that, among the landholders, the status of the *mahattaras* was higher than that of the *kuṭumbis* is perhaps suggested by the combined evidence of Kalaikuri-Sultanpur and Jagadishpur records. In the Kalaikuri-Sultanpur record, the total number of *vīthi-mahattaras* is 8 and that of *kuṭumbis* 76; in the other record it is 4 : 28. Individuals who are seen as having been listed previously in the category of *vīthi-mahattaras* figured, eight years later, as only *kuṭumbis.*[47]

This change in the status of some *vīthi-mahattaras*—from *mahattara* to *kuṭumbi*—has been attributed to their failure to get re-elected to the position they previously held.[48] There are two assumptions behind this suggestion: (1) either the entire rural community as a body or at least the community of landholders elected representatives, of two distinct statuses, to the *vīthi-adhikaraṇa;* (2) such elections were held periodically. The individuals mentioned as *vīthi-mahattaras* and *kuṭumbis* in association with the *vīthi-adhikaraṇa* doubtlessly represented rural landed interests, but it is difficult to substantiate the supposition that a formal elective rural body, with a fixed number of representatives, existed at that time. It is indeed curious that the total number of *vīthi-mahattaras* and *kuṭumbis* is considerably less in the Jagadishpur plate written eight years later than the Kalaikuri-Sultanpur record; if they were elected representatives, one would expect the number of representatives in each category to have remained static in such a short span of time. Moreover, we have suggested earlier that the *vīthi-mahattaras* and *kuṭumbis* may have been associated with the *vīthi-adhikaraṇa,* but they did not constitute it. The fact that another *adhikaraṇa,* the *gramāṣṭakulādhikaraṇa* functioned at a supra-village level along with *kuṭumbis, grāmikas, mahattaras* and brāhmaṇas would perhaps suggest that rural communities associated with such *adhikaraṇas* did not represent formal bodies but were informally structured groups carrying out certain functions which were related to and defined by the functions of the Gupta state. This should explain why the number of *vīthi-mahattaras* and *kuṭumbis* associated with the *vīthi-adhikaraṇa* would vary so considerably within a short span of time. This should further explain the curious fact that while the Kalaikuri-Sultanpur record enumerates one *vīthi-kulika* (member of the artisan community at the *vīthi*-level) and seven *vīthi-kāyasthas* (members of the community of scribes), no member from either community figures at all in the Jagadishpur plate.

It should, in any case, be clear that rural settlements in north Bengal during the Gupta period were neither represented by an all-powerful village headman, nor was there an all-inclusive community organization. But even at the height of its power, the Gupta state accommodated the rural landed interests down to the level of individual villages, though mostly through the mediacy, of supra-village groups representing such interests. This is suggested both by the contents of the communication transmitted to individual villages when plots of land located in them were to be purchased and donated and by the phraseology employed in the records. The Baigram record of 447-8, for example, enjoined those at the rural level who were associated with the work of demarcating a plot of land for sale to see that their own areas of cultivation were not disturbed (*svakarṣaṇāvirodhi-sthāne*).[49] Clearly, the intention conveyed through this expression was that the sale of a plot of land in a village and its subsequent transformation into a tax-free gift land was not to disturb the existing structure of holdings and cultivation arrangements within the village. Second, in most inscriptions of this phase, the actual communication is preceded by the expression *kuśalam-anuvarṇya bodhayanti,* i.e., 'informs after enquiring about their welfare'.[50] The significance of this form of address to social groups at the village is only comprehended when we contrast it with such expressions as *samādiśati* or *samājñāpayati,* i.e. 'commands' or 'orders', which came to be used as major forms of address, conveying communication regarding transfer of land, in inscriptions of later periods.

III

The decline of rural bodies and *adhikaraṇas,* at least at levels at which they interacted mutually as well as with political/administrative tiers above them has, curiously, not received the kind of attention the theme deserves. The theme is of extraordinary significance because it bears upon the nature of the linkage, in early India, between apex political organization and village constituents of the state. By studying the vicissitudes of the rural level organizations of the Gupta period we may hope to arrive at a clearer understanding than we have now of changes in this linkage. Within the frame of this essay it would be impossible to undertake a detailed examination of the stages through which the decline of the rural bodies may be perceived; only select evidence may be presented to understand the processes which started developing from the later phase of Gupta rule in Bengal. In the context of early medieval Tamilnadu, it has been suggested that the autonomy of *nāḍu*-level rural organization of landholders, which was in direct opposition to the state power of the Coḷas, declined as a result of the expansion and consolidation of state power.[51] It is not clear whether this was indeed the historical process operating in rural Tamilnadu in the wake of Coḷa expansion and, further, it does not explain the emergence, in the same political-agrarian context, of the regional *cittirameliperiyanāḍu* or the association of peasant landholders from the twelfth century onward.[52] The decline of the village community is also often attributed to the practice of landgrants which created a layer of landed intermediaries in the rural society and resulted in the corrosion of communal rights in the village.[53] Both are somewhat facile formulations which do not explore the possibility that a section of the rural community could contihue to remain dominant while it was the position of other constituents vis-à-vis the political system which could start undergoing radical changes. To cite an example, epigraphic records make it clear that brāhmaṇas constituted an important community of landholders even in the middle phase of Gupta rule in Bengal, but, at that stage, their position can hardly be distinguished from that of other categories of landholders like non-brāhmaṇa *kuṭumbis* and *mahattaras*. It is only in relation to a later period that the position of the brāhmaṇas as landholders and residents of *agrahāras* can be recognized as distinct.

It has been said above that the political system above the village reached down to its level through different tiers. The tiers may be thus shown:

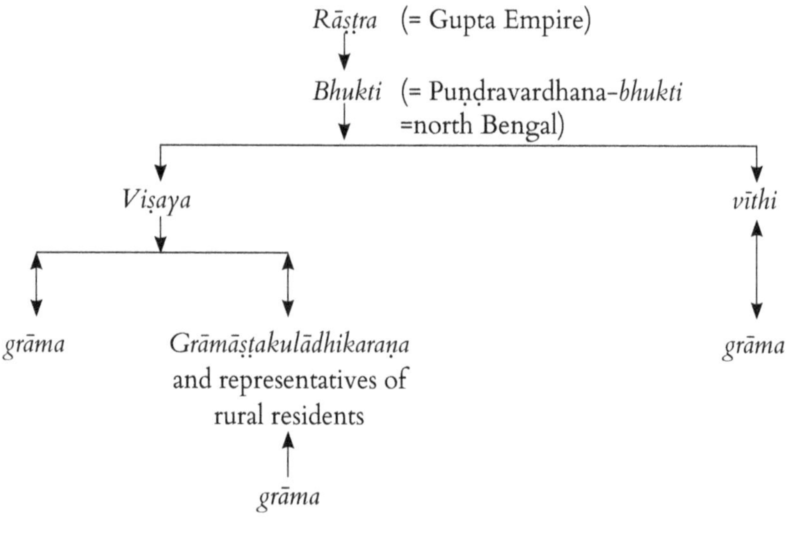

The crucial feature of this arrangement was that there was reciprocal interaction between the tiers down from the *viṣaya* or the equivalent level. In our attempt to analyse the decline of the bodies in which sections of rural community participated, we shall find that it was not only this kind of reciprocal interaction which disappeared, but that the tiers themselves, with their local level executive functions, went out of existence. This of course did not happen suddenly and simultaneously in all areas, and in fact the *adhikaraṇas* at the *viṣaya* or the *vīthi* level continued for a period, although the composition of the *adhikaraṇas* changed in character radically. In some cases, the functions of the *adhikaraṇas* were appropriated by certain new elements. The sixth and seventh centuries constitute a crucial phase for this investigation; we, therefore, need to examine, in detail, some select evidence from these two centuries.

We start with the evidence of the Gunaighar record of AD 507, which, although a record of the late Gupta phase, did not relate to the core region of north Bengal but originated in Comilla area—in what appears to have been a well-settled locality. The inscription,[54] issued from a *jayaskandhāvāra* (camp of victory), was not concerned with the sale of land but with an outright gift of land made on request from a ruler of subordinate status, *mahārāja* Rudradatta. Communication regarding the gift was not conveyed to the village in which the gift land was located but to the *kumārāmātyas* (officials of the rank of a prince) and not by an *adhikaraṇa* at the level of the *viṣaya* but by an individual, *Mahārāja mahāsāmanta* Vijayasena, who is described in the record as *'dūtaka, mahāpratihāra, mahāpilupati, pañcādhikaraṇoparika, pāṭyūparika and purapāloparika'.* In addition to the fact that the record refers to two subordinate rulers under a local Gupta ruler, what ought to strike one as most significant are the appellations of *mahārāja, mahāsāmanta* Vijayasena, one among which was *pañcādhikaraṇāparika. 'Adhikaraṇa'* present in this compound recalls the *adhikaraṇas* of an earlier phase, but *pañcādhikaraṇa* in this case would suggest appropriation of the functions of five *adhikaraṇas* by Vijayasena, an official of important rank under Vainyagupta.

The emergence of the *sāmanta* stratum in the Tripura-Comilla region, therefore, represents a phase in which *adhikaraṇas* of the type found in north Bengal are absent. This, however, was not the case in other regions in which such *adhikaraṇas* are found to have been functioning in the sixth and seventh centuries. It would nevertheless be appropriate to examine in what form they continued to exist. The Mallasarul plate from Burdwan district, also of the sixth century,[55] records a land transaction which was almost identical with land transactions of Gupta period records from north Bengal. Mahārāja Vijayasena, perhaps identical with his namesake of the Gunaighar record, intended, during the reign of Mahārājādhirāja Gopacandra, to make a gift of a plot of land located in the village of Vettragartta within the Vakkattaka *vīthi* of the Vardhamāna *bhukti.* Mahārāja Vijayasena approached various *bhukti* officials as well as *mahattaras* and other landholders for the purchase of the plot, and for our investigation the list of officials at the *bhukti* level and the list of individuals associated with the *vīthi-adhikaraṇa* are worth citing:

1. *Bhukti* officials	*Kārttākṛtika, Kumārāmatya, Cauroddharaṇika, Uparika, Audraṅgika, Agrahārika, Aurṇasthānika, Bhogapati, Viṣayapati, Tadāyuktaka, Hiraṇya-Sāmudāyika, Pattalaka, Avasathika, Devadroṇī-sambaddha.*
2. Individuals associated with *Vakattaka-vīthi-adhikaraṇa*	*Mahattara* Himadatta *agrahārīṇa* of *Ardhakaraka.* *Mahattara* Suvarṇayaśa of Nivṛttavāṭaka. *Mahattara* Dhanasvamī, *agrahārīṇa* of Kapistha-vāṭaka. *Mahattara* Saṣṭhidatta and Śrīdatta, *agrahārīṇa* of Vaṭa-vallaka. *Bhaṭṭa* Vāmanasvamī, *agrahārīṇa* of Koḍḍavīra. Mahīdatta and Rājyadatta, *agrahārīṇa* of Godha*grāma.* Jivasvamī of Śālmalivāṭaka Khāḍgi Hari of Vakkattaka Khāḍgi Goika of Madhuvāṭaka Khāḍgi Bhadranandi of Khaṇḍajoṭika Vāhanāyaka Hari of Vidhyapurī.

Superficially, the format of the Mallasarul record is identical with that of the landsale documents of the Gupta period from north Bengal. The association of individual local landholders with the *vīthi-adhikaraṇa* is similar to what is found in Kalaikuri-Sultanpur and Jagadishpur plates, and the *vīthi-adhikaraṇa* acted as the exclusive office also in this particular transaction. The crucial difference is that communication regarding the sale of the plot of land was neither conveyed to the village Vettra-garttikā in which the land was located nor was Vettra-garttikā represented at the level of the *vīthi-adhikaraṇa* at which landholders from other villages were present. In fact, the composition of both the *vīthi-adhikaraṇa* and of officials at the *bhukti* offers a sharp contrast to what is found in the Gupta records. In place of a representative of the Gupta ruler in charge of *bhukti* administration what we now have is a more elaborate and complex structure constituted by officials of various categories; at the *vīthi,* the representation is from a cluster of settlements of important landholders described as *mahattaras, mahattara-agrahārīṇas* and *agrahārīṇas.* Significantly, the category of *Kuṭumbis* is totally absent. The process of the ascendancy of *mahattaras* and of *sāmantas* is also in evidence in a set of sixth-century inscriptions from the Vaṅga subregion of Bengal. The first plate, of the time of Dharmāditya,[56] records a landsale transaction which started with a request made by a *sādhanika* (official in charge of horses) for the purchase of a plot of land. The request was placed not only before the official in charge of *Vārakamaṇḍala-viṣaya* but also before the *viṣaya-mahattaras* of whom eighteen are mentioned by their names in the record. The *mahattaras* are, thus, seen for the first time functioning at the level of the executive office of a *viṣaya*. Since two other records from Faridpur, belonging to the reigns of Dharmāditya[57] and Gopacandra,[58] mention the *Jyeṣṭha-kāyastha* (corresponding to *prathama-kāyastha* of the Gupta records), in the context of the *Viṣayādhikaraṇa,* it cannot be postulated that the presence of *mahattaras* completely altered the composition of the *viṣayādhikaraṇa* which had, in the Gupta period, consisted of representatives from *Kāyastha, Kulika, Sārthavāha* and *Śreṣṭhi* communities; nevertheless, their dominant presence (indicated by their numerical strength) in the *adhikaraṇa* at the *viṣaya* level is significant. A matter of comparable importance in the Faridpur record of Dharmāditya is that although no *sāmanta* figures in the transaction, it invokes the code of *sāmanta* kings for the protection of the gift land: 'Therefore, the *Sāmanta* kings . . . who have studied the scriptures fully, understanding that "gifts, although given absolutely to persons who rejoice in safeguarding or in discarding gifts of land, must be held valid by those kings" must scrupulously safeguard this gift of land.'[59]

With this may be added that in the Gugrahati plate of Samācāradeva,[60] which originates in the same region and is only slightly later in date, the list of individual *viṣaya-mahattaras* is followed by a general reference to 'many major figures also conversant with the legal code' (*anye ca bahavaḥ pradhāna-vyavahāriṇaśca*).

Two further points may be deduced from the Faridpur plates. One is that like Vettragarttikā of Mallasarul inscription, the villages in which lands, purchased for their transformation into gifts, were located, do not figure in the system of communications. Second, functions like measurement and demarcation of land are no longer carried out by members of the rural community in a representative capacity. Such functions are now carried out by officially appointed individuals like Śivacandra who figures in all three Faridpur plates in connection with measurement of land, or by *kula-vāra* or *jana-kula-vāra* which could be constituted by *Karaṇika* officials.[61] The term *kula-vāra* which occurs in the Mallasarul record, in Faridpur plate (no. 3) and in the Gughrahati record, has been variously but unsatisfactorily interpreted. The term *vāra* which corresponds to *vāra* or *vāriyam* of later records[62] was used in the sense of a body or a committee looking after a particular kind of work, and in *kula* we may find a remnant of the term *aṣṭakula* of the records of the Gupta period. *Kulavāra* then would be something like a body of officials appointed for carrying out certain types of rural work. It was not an informal association existing along with *kuṭumbis, grāmikas,* brāhmaṇas and *mahattaras* at the local, village level but was a formally constituted body at the level of the *viṣaya,* perhaps even at the level of the *bhukti.* This is in keeping with the *mahattaras* also functioning at the level of the *viṣaya* in which, at the stage when the Gughrahati plate was written, the *viṣay-ādhikaraṇa* came to have, instead of representatives from different occupational groups, an obviously important official like *Jyeṣṭhādhikaraṇika.*[63]

The increasing bureaucratization represented by this phase, may merit further probing, but it is another dimension of the evidence that concerns us. The evidence of the Mallasarul record, cited above, suggests that along with a section of non-brāhmaṇa landholders, the brāhmaṇa landholders too, as residents of *agrahāras,* were a dominant group in regions in which the sixth century records are found; this may explain why, in the seventh century during the reign of Śaśāṅka (*c.*AD 600-625), the executive office at Tāvīra (*Tāvīra-karaṇam*) is described in a Midnapore plate as *vipra-pradhāna-saṁgatam.*[64] However, the more detailed evidence of the recently published Egra copperplate of the time of Śaśāṅka from Midnapore district[65] reveals a cross-section of the rural elites of the period: from some new terms like *mahā-mahattara, pradhāna* and *mahāpradhāna,* used in the record, in relation to probably both brāhmaṇa and non-brāhmaṇa landholders, it would appear that the hierarchical ordering of rural landholding elites, present also in the Gupta period, had become much more complex by the seventh century. The inscription records that a number of prominent residents (thirty-five in all) of the locality of Ekatākṣa *viṣaya* (identified with Egra) approached, after receiving a request from a certain official (*antaraṅga*) Doṣatuṅga, the *viṣayādhikaraṇa* which consisted of officials of different categories. The request, as in earlier records, was for the purchase of a plot of uncultivated land measuring 100 *droṇas* located in a village called Kaparddipadraka. The points of relevant interest in the Egra record are: (1) although the majority of the local residents mentioned in the record were not associated, officially or otherwise, with the *adhikaraṇa* of the *viṣaya,* it were they who mediated between the *adhikaraṇa* and the applicant. Individuals who approached the *adhikaraṇa* on *antaraṅga* Doṣatuṅga's behalf in fact belonged either to categories like *mahāmahattara, pradhāna* and *mahāpradhāna* or to official categories like *Karaṇika, Sthāyipāla* and *Pustapāla.* There were, of course, several individuals who did not belong to any of these categories (for details see Appendix 3). So in matter of residence as well as for the total context of this kind of decision-making, it would be difficult to completely separate the two categories, i.e. the category of non-official landholders and the category of officials; (2) of the thirty-five individuals, rank or official designation has been given only for some; others are mentioned along with their village names. Names of at least five *agrahāras* figure in the record, and this, in combination with the evidence of the Mallasarul record, points to the increasing clustering and growing importance of *agrahāra* type settlements and juxtaposition of important landholders of both brāhmaṇa and non-brāhmaṇa communities at the expense of settlements which may have been comparatively insignificant. For example, we have shown that in the Mallasarul record, the village Vettragarttikā in which the gift land was located does not figure in the list of villages or *agrahāras,* representatives from which were involved in the land transaction. The village Kaparddipadraka of Egra plate too does not figure in the list of villages and *agrahāras* whose notable residents mediate between the *viṣayādhikaraṇa* and the purchaser of land which was located in it.

To sum up, what we are trying to argue, on the basis of select evidence chronologically arranged, is this. Although rural stratification and hierarchy of rural settlements did exist in north Bengal in the Gupta period, individual villages were nevertheless recognized as units with which local-level offices could interact, and further, the structure of bodies like *grāmāṣṭakulādhikaraṇa* and *vīthi-adhikaraṇa* ensured participation of rural notables in transactions which concerned rural society. In two centuries following the decline of Gupta power, the composition of those who were associated in executive matters at the levels of *vīthi-adhikaraṇa* and *viṣayādhikaraṇa* seems to have changed considerably as a result of the emergence of new categories of rural notables like *mahā-mahāttara, mahāpradhāna* and so on, as also through the proliferation of *agrahāra*-based brāhmaṇa landholders. Simultaneously, there was a considerable degree of proliferation of officials who came to appropriate much of the functions of the *adhikaraṇas.* By the time of the early phase of Pāla rule in Bengal during eighth and ninth century, even the *adhikaraṇas* at the *viṣaya* level appear to have disappeared, although *viṣaya* as an administrative division continued. The land transfer documents were now no longer concerned with recording various phases which the purchase and subsequent gift of a plot of land involved, but straightaway recorded the communication addressed to officials and different categories of rural residents regarding the gift of land by the ruler. The composition of the groups receiving the address had changed considerably, so had the form of address. The relevant portion of the Khalimpur record of Dharmapāla runs as follows: *Eṣu caturṣu grāmeṣu samupagatān sarvvāneva rāja-rājanaka-rājāputra-rājāmātya-senāpati-viṣayapati-bhogapati-ṣaṣṭhādhikṛta-daṇḍaśakti-daṇḍapāśika-cauroddharaṇika-daussādha-sādhanika-dūta-khola-gamāgamika-abhitvaramāṇa-hastyaśvagom-ahiṣyājāvikādhyakṣa-nākādhyakṣa-balādhyakṣa-tarika-śaulkika-gaulmika-tadāyuktaka-viniyuktādi-rājapādajīvino-nyāṁścākīrtitān-cāṭa-bhāṭajātīyān-yathākālādhyāsino-jyeṣṭhakāyastha-mahāsa-karaṇān prativāsinaḥ kṣetrakarāṁśca brāhmaṇa-mānanā-mahattara-mahattara -daśagrāmikādi-viṣayavyāvahāriṇaḥ pūrvakam yathārham mānayati bodhayati samājñāpayati.*[66] Instead of trying to guess whether all these categories of officials and social groups did actually assemble at the four villages made over to a temple or not, the important point to note is that they were all—and not simply the rural residents of the region—informed about the transfer of land, in this case by *Mahāsāmantādhipati* Nārāyaṇavarman and by *yuvarāja* Tribhuvanapāla who acted as the *dūtaka.* Decisions concerning individual villages had thus come to assume the shape of unilateral, formal administrative decisions which were communicated to officials and local residents priṁarily for the protection of the grants. The grants were to be approved and maintained (*anumodya paripālanīyam*) because they ensured merit, and disturbing them caused 'great sin' (*mahāpātaka*). The residents and cultivators, having received the order, were to provide appropriate dues to the donee. The Khalimpur record lists, among various social groups, *mahāmahattaras* and *mahattaras,* mentioned in earlier records in association with *adhikaraṇas;* they are distinguished from ordinary residents (*prativāsī*) *and* cultivators (*kṣetrakara*), but stratification within individual villages was now overlaid by another hierarchical pattern reflected in the massive proliferation of official designations.

Apart from the growth of different categories of rural notables, some among whom undoubtedly joined the ranks of officials (one may recall this possibility suggested by the Egra plate of Śaśāṅka), there had emerged another situation which must have structured relationships within a number of rural settlements. This situation was caused by a proliferation and clustering of *agrahāra* type of settlements. Inscriptional references to *agrahāras* in Bengal are devoid of such details that can be used for a reconstruction of their internal structure; it is only rarely that one gets a glimpse of how different communities could have been placed within an *agrahāra* society. The Paschimbhag plates of Śrīcandra, issued in the first half of the tenth century in the Śrīhaṭṭa region,[67] offer such a rare glimpse, and we may turn to some of the details in these plates to see how, in a newly created *brahmapura,* different communities were settled, obviously for the purpose of ensuring varieties of services to temples and brāhmaṇas, and how the sizes of plots given to them in return for expected services may reflect the relative social, but not necessarily *varṇa,* statuses of these communities.

The newly created Candrapura-Brahmapura encompassed three *viṣayas* (apparently not administrative divisions in this case) in Śrīhaṭṭa-*maṇḍala*: Garali-*viṣaya,* Pogara-*viṣaya* and Candrapura-*viṣaya.* The large tract of land had apparently not been properly settled since it was given according to *bhūmicchidranyāya.* Second, the manner in which land was distributed among a large number of settlers would further suggest that it was an uncultivated tract. Land in this tract (also called *tri-viṣaya*) was given in three blocks (for details see Appendix 4). In the first block which was attached to a (newly created) temple of Brahmā, the sizes of different plots seem to have been determined in relation to the size of the holding of the brāhmaṇa teacher of *Cāndravyākaraṇa* who received 10 *pāṭakas.* In comparison, the brāhmaṇa who built the temple received only 1 *pāṭaka,* whereas the share of the Kāyastha was 2½ *pāṭakas.* Among the temple servants, the *naṭa* received 2 *pāṭakas* whereas the share of each one of the temple maidservants consisted of ¾ *pāṭakas.* A distinction, which appears to be significant in that it may have derived from a social distinction already in existence, was drawn between two categories of artisan and service communities: while individual carpenters, masons and blacksmiths each received two *pāṭakas* of land, individuals of other communities like *mālākāra, tailika, kumbhakāra, karmmakara, carmakāra* and so on each received only ½ *pāṭaka.* That the sizes of plots were not arbitrarily fixed is clear from specifications regarding the second block of land where too sizes of plots assigned to individual members of these communities were identical. The area of land granted in these two blocks measured 400 *pāṭakas* in all, and the residual land in the three *viṣayas* was distributed among six thousand brāhmaṇas in six thousand equal shares.

The details of land distribution in the Paschimbhag plates may be taken to suggest that in areas where a sizeable population of brāhmaṇas was being settled and temple complexes were being constructed, a society with a largely pre-determined structure could be recreated for making available the services of specialist communities for religious as also non-religious purposes. Further, in trying to understand the structure of mutual relationships between these communities, the model of the *jajmāni* system may be invoked.[68] However, at the most, deductions of a general kind which can be made from the Paschimbhag plates bear upon the relative positions of different communities in rural society in early medieval Bengal. The evidence suggests that there was differentiation even within a supposedly homogenous community and between communities engaged in what would appear to have been analogous professions. While a teacher or a Vedic scholar attached to a *maṭha* was entitled to 10 *pāṭakas* of land, other brāhmaṇas, even of the *mahattara* category, were not entitled to more than 2 *pāṭakas.* This was even less than the shares received by a Kāyastha and a Vaidya whose *varṇa* status was certainly lower than that of the brāhmaṇa. Similarly, carpenters, smiths and artisans were put far above other service communities in terms of their share in land, and although this may be construed to indicate greater relevance of their services for the newly-created *brahmapura,* it is more likely that the differentiated ordering of the various communities in this particular situation derived largely from the pattern of differentiation already in existence in rural society. This is certainly not to suggest that the social and ritual positions of different rural communities were rigidly fixed; that this was not so and that the relative social positions of rural communities could require redefinitions would be clear if one were to refer to the detailed material embedded in Purāṇic and Smṛti works of later periods.[69]

NOTES

1. The occurrence of village names in inscriptions is associated with a single occasion, that is, transfer of land. The epigraphic evidence alone, therefore, is never sufficient for the historical geography of rural settlements, particularly over a long span of time. For distribution of gift land and gift villages mentioned in the inscriptions of Bengal, see B.M. Morrison, *Political Centres and Cultural Regions in Early Bengal,* Tuscon, Arizona, 1970.
2. For a recent thorough analysis of the distribution pattern of pre- and proto-historic sites of West Bengal, see Arun K. Nag, 'Spatial Analysis of Pre- and Proto-historic sites in Ajay-Damodar Valley', in *Archaeology and History: Essays in Memory of A. Ghosh,* ed. B.M. Pande and B.D. Chattopadhyaya, Delhi, 1987, pp. 265-80.
3. O.H.K. Spate, A.T.A. Learmonth and B.H. Farmer, *India, Pakistan and Ceylon: The Regions,* University Paperback edition, Delhi, 1972, p. 590. They, however, admit of exceptions particularly in the 'poorer west' where the terrain appears to favour some concentration.

4. P.C. Chakrabarti in the chapter (xvi) on 'Economic Conditions' in *History of Bengal,* ed. R.C. Majumdar, vol. I, University of Dacca, 1943, p. 643.
5. Niharranjan Ray, *Bangalir Itihas* (in Bengali), 3rd revised edition, Calcutta, 1980, p. 370.
6. Variations in settlement types are however highlighted by others; see Morrison, Introduction; *Rural Settlements in South Asia,* ed. C. Chanana, (Delhi, 1980), passim; *India: A Regional Geography,* ed. R.L. Singh, pp. 272-8.
7. R.G. Basak, 'Dhanaidaha Copperplate Inscription of the Time of Kumaragupta I: the year 113', *EI,* vol. 17, 1923, pp. 345-8.
8. D.C. Sircar, 'Kalaikuri Copperplate Inscription of the Gupta year 120', *The Indian Historical Quarterly,* vol. 19, 1943, pp. 12-26; N.B. Sanyal, 'Sultanpur Copperplate Inscription', *EI,* vol. 31, 1955, pp. 57-66.
9. D.C. Sircar's note in Sanyal, 'Sultanpur Copperplate Inscription'.
10. D.C. Bhattacharyya, 'A Newly Discovered Copperplate from Tipperah', *The Indian Historical Quarterly,* vol. 6, 1930, pp. 45-60; D.C. Sircar, *Select Inscriptions bearing on Indian History and Civilization,* vol. I, University of Calcutta, 2nd edn., 1965, pp. 340-5.
11. Sircar considers the name of the village to be Kāntedadaka-*grāma*; *Select Inscriptions Bearing on Indian History and Civilization,* vol. I, p. 342.
12. For details see Appendix I.
13. The term *Doṣī* has been translated as a cloth merchant on the authority of *Pāio-Sadda-Mahaṇṇavo* (see Anjali Bagai, 'Merchandise and Mercantile community in Post-Gupta Times in Northern India: AD 600-1000' (unpublished Ph.D. Dissertation, Delhi University, 1985), p. 105.
14. L.D. Barnett, 'Vappaghoshavata Grant of Jayanaga', *EI,* vol. 18, 1925-6, pp. 60-4.
15. Ibid.
16. Ibid.
17. The date of Laḍahacandra would be in the first quarter of the eleventh century. Sircar, 'Mainamati Plates of the Chandra Kings', *El,* vol. 38, 1970, pp. 197-214.
18. Ibid., pp. 202-3.
19. Ibid., p. 201.
20. For description of *boro* rice cultivation in the Comilla and other regions see S.H.N. Rizvi, ed., *East Pakistan District Gazetteers: Sylhet,* Dacca, 1970, pp. 126-7; Nurul Islam Khan, ed., *Bangladesh District Gazetteers: Comilla,* Dacca, 1977, p. 77.
21. N.G. Majumdar, *Inscriptions of Bengal,* vol. 3, Rajshahi, 1929, pp. 132-9; line 42 of Madanpada plate.
22. This suggestion occurs in D.C. Sircar, 'Madanpada plate of Visvarupasena', *EI,* vol. 33, Delhi, 1959-60, pp. 315-16.
23. R.G. Basak, 'Tipperah Copperplate Grant of Lokanātha: the 44th year', *EI,* vol. 15, 1919-20, pp. 301-15.

24. 'Paschimbhag plate of Śrīcandra, regnal year 5', in *Epigraphic Discoveries in East Pakistan*, D.C. Sircar, Calcutta, 1973, pp. 19–40, 63–9.
25. D.C. Sircar, 'Śaśāṅker rājatvakālīna Egrā tāmraśāsana' (in Bengali), reprinted from *Sahitya Parishat Patrika,* no. 4, year 87, pp. 1-5. The Egra plate dates to the seventh century.
26. Basak, 'Tipperah Copperplate Grant of Lokanātha'.
27. 'Bhuvaneswar Inscription of Bhaṭṭa Bhavadeva', N.G. Majumdar, *Inscriptions of Bengal,* p. 40, verse 26.
28. F. Kielhorn, 'Khalimpur plate of Dharmapāladeva', *EI,* vol. 4, 1896-7, pp. 253–8; R. Mukherji and S.K. Maity, *Corpus of Bengal Inscriptions bearing on History and Civilization of Bengal,* Calcutta, 1967, pp. 95–109.
29. D.C. Sircar, *Epigraphic Discoveries in East Pakistan,* pp. 19–40, 63–9. The following identifications for the rivers and channels, constituting boundaries of the donated tract, have been suggested: (i) Kosiyara = Kusiyara river; (ii) Mani-nadi = Manu river; (iii) Jujju = Jujnachara canal; (iv) Vetraghanghi = Ghunghi river. All are located in Sylhet district; ibid., p. 31.
30. Basak, 'Tipperah Copperplate Grant of Lokanātha'.
31. 'Naihati Copperplate of Vallalasena', in *Inscriptions of Bengal,* N.G. Majumdar, pp. 68–80.
32. K.N. Dikshit, 'Paharpur Copperplate Grant of [Gupta] Year 159', *EI,* vol. 20, 1929–30, pp. 59–64.
33. Apart from local administrative centres covering several villages, the combination of two or more villages for the purpose of organizing a revenue unit may perhaps be noticed in several Gupta inscriptions; cf. for example the evidence of the Kalaikuri-Sultanpur record of 440-1 from Raishahi district, which refers to the villages Tāpasapottaka and Dayitapottaka in the *prāveśya* of Vibhītaka, N.B. Sanyal, 'Sultanpur Copperplate Inscription' for the meaning of *prāveśya,* taken to suggest combination of villages for revenue assessment see D.C. Sircar's note, ibid., p. 59 fn 1.
34. 'Sunderban Copperplate of Lakshmanasena', in *Inscriptions of Bengal,* Majumdar, pp. 169–72.
35. Basak, 'Dhanaidaha Copperplate Inscription of the Time of Kumaragupta I: The year 118'.
36. R.G. Basak, 'The Five Damodarpur Copperplate Inscriptions of the Gupta Period', *EI,* vol. 15, 1919–20, pp. 113–45; plate no. 3.
37. R.G. Basak, Baigram Copperplate Inscription of the Gupta Year 128', *EI,* vol. 21, 1931-32, pp. 78–83.
38. Ibid., p. 81.
39. *Aṣṭakulādhikaraṇa* would, in the literal sense, imply the institution of an *adhikaraṇa* or office by representatives from eight families. The term is comparable to *aṭṭhakulaka* which occurs in the *Mahāpariṇibbāṇasutta* in the context of the administration of justice in Vaiśālī; R. Fick, *The Social Organization in Northeast India in Buddha's time,* tr. S.K. Maitra, University of Calcutta, 1920, Chap. 4.

40. Toshio Yamazaki, 'Some Aspects of Landsale Inscriptions in Fifth and Sixth Century Bengal', *Acta Asiatica,* no. 43 (Japanese Studies in Ancient and Medieval Indian History), Tokyo, 1982, pp. 17-36.
41. See Morrison, *Political Centres and Cultural Regions,* Chap. 5.
42. Sanyal, 'Sultanpur Copperplate Inscription'.
43. Sircar, *Epigraphic Discoveries from East Pakistan,* pp. 8-14, 61-3.
44. See note 35.
45. See notes 41 and 42.
46. See Appendix 2 of this volume.
47. For a discussion of textual and other references to *Kuṭumbins* and *Mahattaras,* Yamazaki, 'Some Aspects of Landsale Inscriptions in Fifth and Sixth Century Bengal', pp. 24-30.
48. Sircar, *Epigraphic Discoveries in East Pakistan,* p. 10.
49. Basak, 'Baigram Copperplate Inscription of the Gupta Year 128'.
50. Ibid., also cf. the expression *'Kuśalamuktvānudarśayanti . . . Vijñāpayati* in Damodarpur Copperplate of 482–83, no. 3; R.G. Basak, 'The Five Damodarpur Copperplate Inscriptions of the Gupta Period', p. 136.
51. K.R. Hall, *Trade and Statecraft,* passim.
52. For *cittirameli-periyanāḍu* see K.G. Krishnan, *Studies in South Indian History and Epigraphy,* Madras, 1981, pp. 59-66.
53. R.S. Sharma, 'How Feudal was Indian Feudalism?, op. cit.
54. Sircar, *Select Inscriptions bearing on Indian History and Civilization,* pp. 340-5.
55. Majumdar, 'Mallasarul Copperplate of Vijayasena', *EI,* vol. 23 (1935-36), pp. 155-61.
56. F.E. Pargiter, 'Three copperplate grants from East Bengal', *The Indian Antiquary,* vol. 39, 1910, pp. 193-216.
57. Ibid.
58. Ibid.
59. The translation of the passage in Pargiter is not entirely satisfactory; he translates *sāmantarāja* as 'the kings who are neighbours to the above-mentioned grant', ibid., p. 198. The relevant passage runs as follows: *Tadupari-likhi-tak-āgama-sāmanta-rājabhiḥ samadhigata-śāstrabhir-bhūmidān-anupālana-kṣep-anumodaneṣu samyag-dat-tāny-api dānāni rājabhir-anyaiḥ pratipāda-nīyāniti . . .*
60. N.K. Bhaṭṭasali, 'The Ghughrahati Copperplate Inscription of Samacharadeva', *EI,* vol. 18, 1925-6, pp. 74-86.
61. Cf. the expression *Karaṇika-Nayanāga-Keśavādin-Kula-vārān-prakalpya* in the Ghughrahati record of Samachara-deva, ibid., p. 77.
62. For *vāriyams* in south Indian *sabhās* see K.A. Nilakanta Sastri, *The Coḷas,* pp. 494-6; Burton Stein, *Peasant State and Society in Medieval South India,* p. 145 ff.; the term *vāra* occurs in the ninth-tenth century Gurjara-Pratihāra documents from Siyadoni; F. Kielhorn, 'Siyadoni Stone Inscription', *EI,* vol. I, Calcutta, 1892, p. 173.
63. Bhaṭṭasali, 'The Ghughrahali, Copper Plate Inscription of Samacharaderea'.

64. Majumdar, 'Two Copperplates of Śaśāṅka from Midnapore', *Journal of the Asiatic Society of Bengal,* Letters, vol. II, 1945, pp. 1-9.
65. Sircar, 'Sasanker Rajatvakalina Egra Tamraśāsana'.
66. F. Kielhorn, 'Khalimpur Plate of Dharmapāladeva'; lines 43-47 and Kielhorn's translation.
67. Sircar, *Epigraphic Discoveries in East Pakistan,* pp. 19-40, 63-9.
68. For *jajmāni* system see W.H. Wiser, *The Hindu Jajmani System*, Lucknow, 1936. However, Wiser's stress on equal dependence has been criticized by Beidelman who provides a different definition of the *jajmāni* system: 'The *jajmani* system is a feudalistic system of prescribed, hereditary obligations of payment and of occupational and ceremonial duties between two or more specific families of different castes in the same locality', T.O. Beidelman, *A Comparative Analysis of the Jajmani System,* New York: 1959, p. 6.

    For evidence comparable to what is available in the Paschimbhag Plates in such texts as the *Skandapurāṇa* see B.N.S. Yadava, *Society and Culture in Northern India in the Twelfth Century,* Allahabad, 1973, pp. 164-5. Modern parallel where *adimai* services were provided to distinct brahmin lineages can be found in a detailed study of Kumbapettai village of Tanjore district: see Kathleen Gough, 'Caste in a Tanjore village' in *Aspects of Caste in South India, Ceylon and Northwest Pakistan*, ed. Edmund Leach, Cambridge, 1960, pp. 11-60; Idem, *Rural Society in Southeast India,* 1981, p. 178 ff.

    There are, however, several points arising from the evidence of the Paschimbhag plates which should warn us against a too facile comparison with the *jajmāni* system as also against accepting the system as a universal mode of interaction between segments in a village society. First, the direction of the flow of services is implicit in the record but is a one-way channel; it is not at all clear what type of reciprocity is intended. Second, the total size of the communities expected to provide services is inadequate for the complex of *maṭhas* and the community of brāhmaṇas With their juxtaposed presence at Candrapura *śāsana*, it seems that the services were intended only for the *maṭhas,* leaving it uncertain as to how services for the brāhmaṇa settlement, were to be acquired. Third, the relationship between a community and the service it provided to the village society may have remained stable, but the conditions of service in a newly created settlement were not necessarily identical with those in a settled area even when the latter could be converted into a grant area.
69. See Ray, *Bangalir Itihas,* chap. 6.

Appendix 1

Boundary-Specifications in the Gunaighar Record of the Time of Vainyagupta, GE 188 (= 507 AD)

Lines 18-31: 'Wherein the first plot of land measuring seven *Pāṭakas* and nine *Droṇavāpas* [*Yattr = aika-kṣettra-khaṇḍe nava-droṇavāpādhika-saptapāṭaka-parimāṇe*] the boundary-marks are: to the East, the border of Guṇikāgrahāra village and the field [*kṣettra*] of *vardhaki* [*carpenter*] Viṣṇu; to the South, the field of Miduvilāla (?) and the field belonging to the Royal *vihāra* [*Rājavihāra*]; to the West, the Sūrī-Nāśī-Rampūraṇeka-*Kṣetram*; to the north, the tank [*puṣkariṇī*] in the enjoyment [*bhoga*] of Doṣī . . . and the boundaries of the fields of Piyāka and Ādityabandhu.

Of the second plot measuring twenty-eight *Droṇavāpas* the boundaries are: to the east, border of Guṇikāgrahāra village; to the south, the field of Pakkavilāla(?); to the west, the field of the Royal *vihāra*; to the north, the field of Vaidya. . . .

Of the third plot measuring twenty-three *Droṇavāpas* the boundaries are: to the east, the field of . . . ; to the south, the boundary limit of the field of Makhadvārchharika; to the west, the field of Jolārī; to the north, the field of Nāgī Jodāka.

Of the fourth plot of land measuring thirty *Droṇavāpas,* the boundaries are: to the east, the boundary limit of the field of Buddhāka; to the south, the field of Kālāka; to the west, the boundary limit of the field of Sūryya; to the north, the field of Mahīpāla.

Of the fifth plot of land measuring a couple of *Pāṭakas* less a quarter, the boundaries are: to the east, the *Khaṇḍaviḍuggurika-kṣetra*; to the south, the field of Maṇibhadra, to the west, the boundary limit of the field of Yajñarāta; to the north, the boundary limit of the village Nāda-udaka.

* This extract is in most parts from D.C. Bhattacharya, 'A newly discovered copperplate from Tippera', *The Indian Historical Quarterly,* vol. 6, 1930, pp. 45-60. However, in modifying Bhattacharya's translation and inserting original expressions, when required, D.C. Sircar's text of the inscription (*Select Inscriptions bearing on Indian History and Civilization,* vol. I, pp. 340-5) has been used.

The boundary-marks of the lowlands [*tala-bhūmi*] belonging to the *vihāra* are: to the east, the ditch [*jolā*] between the (two) landing places of boats at Cūḍāmaṇi and Nagaraśrī [*Cuḍāmaṇi-Nagaraśrī-nauyogayor-madhye*]; to the south, the channel open to boats connected to the tank of Gaṇeśvara-vilāla; to the west, the end of the field belonging to the temple of Pradyumeneśvara; to the north, the channel leading to the landing place of boats at Praḍāmāra [*Praḍāmāranauyoga-Khātaḥ*].

The boundary marks also of the *hajjika-khila-bhūmi* at the entrance of the *vihāra* . . . are: to the east, the boundary limit of the field belonging to the temple of Pradyumneśvāra; to the south, the limit of the field belonging to the *vihāra* of the Buddhist monk Ācārya Jitasena; to the west, the stream [*gaṁga*] Hacāta; to the north, the tank [*puṣkariṇī*] of Daṇḍa.'

Appendix 2

Lists of Vīthi-mahattaras, Kuṭumbis and others in Kalaikuri-Sultanpur (AD 440) and in Jagadishpur (AD 447) Copperplates

KALAIKURI-SULTANPUR PLATE[1]	JAGADISHPUR PLATE[2]
Vīthi-Kulika	*Vīthi-mahattara*
1. Bhīma	1. Kumāradeva
	2. Gaṇḍa
Kāyastha	3. Prajāpati
1. Prabhucandra	4. Jyeṣṭhadāma
2. Rudradāsa	
3. Devadatta	*Kuṭumbi*
4. Lakṣmaṇa	1. Yaśoviṣṇu
5. Kāntideva	2. Umayaśas
6. Śambhudatta	3. Hariśarman
7. Kṛṣṇadāsa	4. Sarpapālita
	5. Hiraṇyagupta
Pustapāla	6. Kumārayaśas
1. Siṁhanandi	7. Kumārabhūti
2. Yaśodāma	8. Śivakuṇḍa
	9. Śiva
Vīthi-mahattara	10. Śiva
1. Kumāradeva	11. Somaviṣṇu
2. Gaṇḍa	12. Satyaviṣṇu
3. Prajāpati	13. Kaṅkutti
4. Umayaśa	14. Nandadāman
5. Rāmaśarma	15. Vīranāga
6. Jyeṣṭhadāma	16. Nārāyaṇadāsa
7. Svāmicandra	17. Rudra

[1] N.B. Sanyal, 'Sultanpur Copperplate Inscription', *EI*, 31, pp. 57-66.
[2] D.C. Sircar, *Epigraphic Discoveries in East Pakistan*, pp. 8-14, 61-3.

KALAIKURI–SULTANPUR PLATE	JAGADISHPUR PLATE
Kuṭumbi	18. Bhava
1. Yaśoviṣṇu	19. Guha
2. Kumāraviṣṇu	20. Acyuta
3. Kumārabhāva	21. Kubera
4. Kumārabhūti	22. Sarvanāga
5. Kumāra	23. Bhavanāga
6. Yaśogupta	24. Śrīdatta
7. Vailinandi?	25.Bhavadatta
8. Śivakuṇḍa	26. Dhanaviṣṇu
9. Vasuśiva	27. Guṇaratha
10. Aparaśiva	28. Naradeva
11. Dāmarudra	
12. Prabhumitra	
13. Kṛṣṇamitra	
14. Maghaśarmma	
15. Īśvaracandra	
16. Rudra	
17. Bhavanātha	
18. Śrīnātha	
19. Hariśarmma	
20. Guptaśarmma	
21. Suśarmma	
22. Hari	
23. Alātasvāmī	
24. Brahmasvāmī	
25. Mahāsenabhaṭṭa	
26. Saṣṭhīrāma	
27. Gu . . . śarmma	
28. Untaśarmma	
29. Kṛṣṇadatta	
30. Nandadāma	
31. Bhavadatta	
32. Ahiśarmma	
33. Somaviṣṇu	
34. Lakṣmaṇaśarmma	
35. Dhaivvaka?	
36. Kṣemaśarmma	
37. Sakkraśarmma	
38. Sarpapālita	
39. Kaṅkuṭi	
40. Viśva-śaṅkara	
41. Jayasvāmī	
42. Kaivarttaśarmma	
43. Himaśarmma	

KALAIKURI–SULTANPUR PLATE
44. Purandara
45. Jayaviṣṇu
46. Jayaviṣṇu
47. Uma . . .
48. Simhadatta
49. Bonda
50. Nārāyaṇadāsa
51. Vīranāga
52. Rājyanāga
53. Guha
54. Mahī
55. Bhavanātha
56. Guhaviṣṇu
57. Sarvva
58. Yaśoviṣṇu
59. Takka
60. Kuladāma
61. . . . va-Śrī
62. Guhaviṣṇu
63. Rāmasvāmī
64. Kamanakuṇḍa
65. Ratibhadra
66. Acyutabhadra
67. Lodhaka
68. Prabhakīrtti
69. Jayadatta
70. Kaluka?
71. Acyuta
72. Naradeva
73. Bhava
74. Bhavarakṣita
75. Piccakuṇḍa
76. Pravarakuṇḍa
77. Sarvvadāsa
78. Gopāla

Appendix 3

List of Important Landholders and Officials Resident in Ekatākakṣa-viṣaya (Egra),[1] Midnapore District, in the Seventh Century

Mahāmahattara Skandasena and Nāgasena of Ekatākakṣa
Paṭa of the *agrahāra* of (?)
Nāgadeva and Anantadeva of the *agrahāra* of Trāṇeka
Mahāmahattara Dharmagupta and Yājñavasu of Taraktodarbha *agrahāra*
Mahāmahattara Somadeva and Guhadeva of Loḍḍāvā *agrahāra*
Mahāmahattara Godhyakṣighoṣa and Mokṣadeva of Ākhavaṭayika *agrahāra*
Mahāmahattara Mahībhadra, Rāta and Chātra of Vimśatikhaḍḍāna
Mahattara Gomidatta of Mṛgātā
Bhaṭṭa Dhanapala of Gurjārapadraka
Bhaṭṭa Gopāladeva of Kāpalāśaka
Mahādeva of Sarṣapavāsinī
Raithisvāmī of Brāhmaṇapadraka
Vaiṣayika Anāma
Mahāmahattara Vatsaśarmā
Mahāpradhāna Udayacandra
Pradhāna Jayadeva
Pradhāna Dhruvada
Pradhāna Yaśonāga
Pradhāna Bāndhavanāga
Karaṇikas Pravṛddhadatta, Samudradatta and Uddyotasiṁha
Pustapālas Jinasena, Ādāmara and Acona
Sthāyipālas Śrīdharma and Svasti

[1] D.C. Sircar, 'Śaśāṅker Rājatvakālīna Egra Tāmraśāsana', *Sahitya Parisat Patrika,* no. 4, year 87, pp. 1-5; see also, D.C. Sircar, 'Indological Notes', *Journal of Ancient Indian History,* vol. 12, 1978-9, pp. 132-7.

Appendix 4

Landshares as Specified in the Paschimbhag Plates of Śrī Candra, Regnal Year 5 (*c.*AD 930)

1. First block attached to the *maṭha* (monastery) of Brahmā?
   10 *Pāṭakas* (each measuring 10 *droṇas*) to teacher (*upādhyāya*) of *Cāndravyākaraṇa*
   10 *Pāṭakas* for the maintenance of 10 students
   5 *Pāṭakas* for the daily offering of food to 5 guest brāhmaṇas
   1 *Pāṭaka* to the brāhmaṇa who built the temple
   1 *Pāṭaka* to the astrologer (*gaṇaka*)
   2½ *Pāṭakas* to Kāyastha
   ½ *Pāṭaka* to each one of:
   (1) 4 florists (*mālākāra*)
   (2) 2 oil pressers (*tailika*)
   (3) 2 potters (*Kumbhakāra*)
   (4) 5 players of drum called *Kahala*
   (5) 2 conchshell blowers (*śaṅkha-vādaka*)
   (6) 2 players on big drum called *ḍhakka*
   (7) 8 players on kettle-drum (*dragada*)
   (8) 22 *Karmmakaras* (servants)[1] and leather-workers (*carmmakāra*)
   2 *Pāṭakas* to the dancer (*Naṭa*)
   2 *Pāṭakas* to each of:
   (1) 2 carpenters (*sūtradhara*)
   (2) 2 masons (*sthapati*)
   (3) 2 blacksmiths (*Karmakāra*)
   ¾ *Pāṭaka* to each of 8 maidservants (*ceṭikā*)
   47 *Pāṭakas* for repairs (*navakarman*) of the temple establishment.
2. Second block of land given in favour of deities Vaiśvānara, Yogeśvara, Jaimani, and Mahākāla, worshipped in four *deśāntarīya* (non-local) and four *Vaṅgāla* (local) *maṭhas.*

* *Source:* D.C. Sircar, *Epigraphic Discoveries in East Pakistan,* Calcutta, 1973, pp. 31-6, 63-9.

[1] *Karmmakaras* may also refer to agricultural workers.

10 *Pāṭakas* to each one of 8 teachers of 4 *Vedas*
5 *Pāṭakas* to each group of 5 students in 8 *maṭhas*
½ *Pāṭaka* to each one of the following in 8 *maṭhas:*

(1) florist
(2) barber (*nāpita*)
(3) oil-presser
(4) washerman (*rajaka*)
(5) 8 servants (*Karmmakara*) and leatherworkers.

¾ *Pāṭaka* to each of 2 maidservants (*ceṭṭikā*) in 8 *maṭhas.*
10 *Pāṭakas* for repairs to each one of 8 *maṭhas*
2 *Pāṭakas* to *mahattara* Brāhmaṇas in each of 2 groups of *maṭhas*
2½ *Pāṭakas* to Kāyasthas of each of the 2 groups of *maṭhas*
1 *Pāṭaka* to the astrologer (*gaṇaka*) of each of the 2 groups of *maṭhas.*
3 *Pāṭakas* to the physician (*vaidya*) of each of the 2 groups of *maṭhas*
1½ *Pāṭakas* to the superintendent (*vārika*) of each of the 2 groups of *maṭhas.*

3. The third block of land, which was the leftover in the region called Triviṣaya where the Candrapura-Brahmapura was created, was given to 6,000 brāhmaṇas in 6,000 equal shares. From the total area, only 52 *pāṭakas* (measuring 10 *droṇas* each) of land attached to Indreśvara's boat station (*Indreśvara-naubandha-pratibaddha*) were excluded.

Three

Villages, Wells and Rulers in South-Eastern Marwar: Aspects of Rural Settlements and Rural Society in the Kingdom of the Nadol Cāhamānas

THE REGIONAL FOCUS of this essay is on south-eastern Marwar in western Rajasthan. An attempt will be made here to examine some aspects of rural settlements in the kingdom of the Cāhamānas of Nadol, the core area of which was located in what was previously known as the Godwad division of Marwar.[1] Comprising the Bali and Desuri tehsils of the present Pali district, the semi-arid Godwad division corresponds to a tract along and to the west of the Aravalli range which separates Marwar from Mewar, through which, however, exist passes connecting the two regions.[2] Before we state the main concerns of this essay, we may point to some of the limitations in its scope. The essay is concerned with the Nadol Cāhamāna kingdom but not with the entire period of Nadol Cāhamāna history which, if we consider the Jalor Cāhamānas as well, continued down to the fourteenth century.[3] The inscriptional material examined here ranges in time from the close of the eleventh to the close of the twelfth century, the rationale for this choice of chronology being that the few aspects of early medieval rural settlements that we propose to examine can be so done by taking together the epigraphs of this period. At the same time, rural settlements of south-east Marwar, as elsewhere, although not altogether anonymous, figure in inscriptions only in the contexts of various types of grants as bases from which resources were being transferred. The inscriptions capture 'particular events' of certain villages by recording how on a specified occasion certain resources were being transferred, and we cannot really expect to reconstruct, on the basis of such evidence, a detailed history of villages or of their social structures over a period of about hundred years. Dictated by the nature of the evidence, the main themes that will be taken up hare are: (1) the nature of the village resources and of their redistribution, (2) the relationship of villages with what may be called their nodes, and (3) the nature of pressure which the internal structure of Nadol Cāhamāna polity may have generated in the distribution of villages and village lands.

I

The Nadol Cāhamāna kingdom came into existence toward the close of the tenth century through adventurous initiatives taken by Lakṣmaṇa who was seemingly legendary but apparently a historical figure.[4] He figures in the genealogies provided by the inscriptions of the later rulers of the line as a son of Śākambharī Cāhamāna Vākpatirāja, who branched off from the main Cāhamāna family and founded a new kingdom.[5] As Rāval Lakhā of tradition, incorporated in such texts as *Purātanaprabandha-saṁgraha* and Nainsi's *Khyāt,* he set off from Śākambharī with only two companions, protected the brāhmaṇas of Nadol from the depredations of the Meḍas, gradually built up a band of followers and acquired resources necessary for ruling the region. What we really seem to have here, in the references to the heroic protection which Lakṣmaṇa extended to the brāhmaṇas against the depredations of the hostile Meḍas, in the fantastic account of how Lakhā acquired a huge cavalry and in similar other stories, is another instance of the colonization of a tribal tract by a ruling family which needed to expand. There are instances of this kind from an earlier period;[6] the history of the Nadol Cāhamānas provides examples of expansion, including expansion of this kind.[7] The Godwad tract was not totally barren at this time. Two inscriptions, one of the early tenth and the other of the late tenth century from Bijapur in the extreme south-east of Marwar, refer to a Rāṣṭrakūṭa kingdom at Hastikuṇḍikā (Hathundi) in which *araghaṭṭa* irrigation in its rural hinterland, producing wheat, barley, pulses and cotton, was already in vogue.[8] Hastikuṇḍikā also appears to have been a centre of exchange of some importance.[9] The upper parts of the Godwad plain thus offered sufficient attraction for a fresh team of colonizers. Nadol, or Naḍḍula as it is called in the inscriptions, was the centre of this new kingdom until the time when Nadol Cāhamāna capital was shifted to the fortified hill capital of Suvarṇagiri or Jalor. Two inscriptions of the time of Lakṣmaṇa, dated 967 and 982,[10] were reported but never published, and the kingdom of Nadol really came into the focus of history only from the close of the eleventh century, about a hundred years after the time of Lakṣmaṇa. It was variously called Naḍḍuladeśa of Naḍḍulamaṇḍala,[11] but the *deśa* or the *maṇḍala* did not designate fixed political boundaries. It essentially designated the cote region of the territories held by the Nadol Cāhamānas, which could vary from one period of time to another, and in periods of large-scale expansion, Naḍḍula was distinguished from other territorial units.[12] This point should underline the close linkage between the Nadol Cāhamānas and the region of Nadol as their domain, even though in periods when the Cāhamānas acknowledged the suzerainty of the Caulukyas of Gujarat, Nadol was declared to have been received by them as a favour from the Caulukyas.[13] The point of reference for examining the agrarian arrangements in Nadol should, therefore, be the Cāhamānas of Nadol and not the Caulukyas of Gujarat, and it is by referring to Nadol as the domain of the Cāhamānas that we propose to examine the inscriptional material bearing on the early medieval rural settlements of south-eastern Marwar.

II

We begin by trying to understand how the villages, the village wells[14] and the cultivators figure in the inscriptions. Although villages figure only incidentally in the contexts of grants—grants of fields, of entire villages, of village resources either in the form of shares in their products or in cash or, in exceptional cases, in the form of the cultivators themselves—several points nevertheless emerge from a study of these grants. To reiterate a point made earlier, the earliest inscriptional records of any importance appear only about hundred years after the establishment of the Nadol Cāhamāna kingdom by Lakṣmaṇa, and this may suggest that the process of the crystallization of rural settlements and of the practice of transferring resources from them was not necessarily conterminous with the foundation of the kingdom: we are not suggesting complete absence of either but a possible change in scale over a period of hundred years.

The earliest example of such transfer from the region comes from the Sevadi stone inscription of the time of Aśvarāja (1110).[15] The inscription records the transfer of one *hāraka* of barley per *arahaṭa* from the villages of Padrada, Medraṁca, Chechaḍiyā and Maḍḍāḍi for the daily worship of Śrī Dharmanāthadeva at the temple of Samīpāṭī or Sevadi. The transfer was made not by the king or the Yuvarāja who was assigned the town of Samīpāṭī for his enjoyment but by the 'Great master of stables' (*mahā-sāhaniya*) Uppalarāka, along with members of his family, some of whom are named in the inscription. The question of the distribution of rural settlements in terms of who enjoyed and transferred their resources will be taken up later, but for the moment only the points, arising out of the Sevadi record and other similar records, relating to the nature of rural settlements may be noted. The resources to be transferred from the villages are expressed, in the Sevadi inscription, in terms of *arahaṭas* or *araghaṭṭas* or irrigation wells. In fact, in the records of the region in general *araghaṭṭas* figure regularly in contexts which mention rural settlements. The expression *arahaṭam arahaṭam prati*, i.e. per *arahaṭa* is significant in terms of the fact that it underlines the link between the well and agricultural production, for *araghaṭṭa* signified both well and the area of land which was irrigated by it. *Araghaṭṭas* were given individual identities in the form of names, with or without reference to the fields they cultivated. The Bali stone inscription of the time of Aśvarāja (called Āśvāka in this inscription, dated 1143),[16] while giving details of financial arrangements made for the *Yātrā* of the deity Bahughṛṇādevī at the village Bālahiya (Bālahiya *grāma,* modern Bali) which incidentally was being enjoyed at that time by queen Tihaṇukā as a *grāsa,* specifies contributions, assessed in cash, from the *araghaṭṭas* 'Sitka, Bhoria, Bohada, Mahiya' and others. The Lalrai stone inscription, of 1176, of the time of Kelhaṇa, specified one *hāraka* of barley, according to the system of measure in vogue in Gurjaratṛ, from an *araghaṭṭa* called Urahāri belonging to the village of Bhaḍiyāuva.[17]

It would be impossible to calculate how much of an area in a village could be irrigated by *araghaṭṭas* or the exact number of *araghaṭṭas* a village was likely to have. The Bali stone inscription of 1143, cited earlier,[18] shows that the village of Bālahiya or Bali had certainly more than four *araghaṭṭas;* two inscriptions from Lalrai, both dated 1176, refer to two different *araghaṭṭas* at the village of Bhadiyauva.[19] The distribution pattern of wells, even in such a small region, appears to have been varied, their incidence depending on both environmental and institutional factors. The types of wells too varied. The nature of the difference between types is not made clear in the inscriptions, but a broad distinction is nevertheless present in the inscriptions in the use of two expressions: (1) *ḍhiku* or *ḍhiṁka* and (2) *araghaṭṭa.* There are cases where both expressions figure in the same record.[20] *Ḍhiku* is explained away either as 'a well as distinguished from an *araghaṭṭa*'[21] or 'as a well irrigating about half as much land as an *araghaṭṭa.*[22] Whatever the exact meaning of the term[23] and its difference from an *araghaṭṭa,*[24] a set of three records from Bamnera,[25] relating to a settlement called Koraṁṭaka and referring to both *ḍhiku* and *arahaṭa,* permits us a close look at the relationship between well irrigation, fields under cultivation and the practice of land grants. The first record, dated 1163, refers to a *ḍohalikā,* i.e. a plot of land given to a brahmin who in this case was a brahmin called Nārāyaṇa.[26] The plot was located between four other plots (*kṣetram*) held by different individuals, and somewhat curiously no well is mentioned in the context of any of the plots specified in this record. The second record, dated 1164, however, refers simply to the grant to the same brahmin of a *ḍhiku* or a well but it must be taken to mean that a plot of land with a well in it was given, for the location of the well as specified in the record would suggest that it was not on the plot (*ḍohalikā*) previously given to the brahmin. On its east was located another *ḍhiku* or well belonging to another brāhmaṇa; on its west was an *arahaṭa* called *Duḍādua;* on the north was another well belonging to the deity Vyāsanarabrahmadeva and on the south too was a well belonging to the deity Mahāsvāmī. The third, an undated inscription, records another grant of a well to the same brāhmaṇa, and its boundaries were: river to the east and the north; a well called *Rāṇala-ḍhiku* to the west and the well belonging to the deity Mahāsvāmī, mentioned earlier in the second record, to the south.

The rather obvious points which emerge from the usually neglected details cited above are these. At Koraṁṭaka the incidence of wells was high, although wells are not mentioned in the context of all cultivated plots which figure in the records. It would seem significant that increasingly better provisions were made for the brāhmaṇa donee; his first plot of land did not have any well in it but the two other plots which were added to his holdings at subsequent stages were located in areas with adequate irrigation facilities, including channels to carry water from the wells. One of the later records carries the stipulation that 'the channel should not be damaged'.[27] Even in an area with great irrigation potential, it seems then that there existed two types of land and perhaps a corresponding difference among those among whom these types of land were distributed. At Koraṁṭaka, of the seven wells which figure in the records, six belonged either to the brāhmaṇas or to the deities.

Koraṁṭaka, however, need not be taken as a typical rural settlement of the region. Probably located along the river Jawai, vhich is the most plausible identification of the river mentioned in the third record as forming the boundary of cultivated plots,[28] its conditions of agriculture may have differed to a considerable degree from those of other settlements in the region. The evidence from Koraṁṭaka may nevertheless be taken to provide a preliminary idea of the social layers which epigraphs only rarely and partly reveal but which need to be considered together for reconstructing an overview of the agrarian structure of the Godwad region. The act of the transfer of land to a brahmin donee took place in the kingdom of the Nadol Cāhamānas whose representatives were present to ratify the act, but Koraṁṭaka itself was located in what may be called an assignment (*sejā*) of a local ruling family.[29] The other donees with plots already assigned to them were several deities in local shrines. At the same time, the records allude to other segments of rural society by specifying plots held individually at Koraṁṭaka and to the admixture of such plots with those given to brāhmaṇas and deities. Evidence from other settlements too would suggest varied social composition of rural settlements and indicate the existence of a local landholding stratum. At a general level, an impression to this effect is conveyed by the compound expression *mahājana-grāmīṇa-janapada-samakṣa* which occurs in a Nadlai inscription of 1143 of the time of Rāyapāla.[30] This local resident stratum in rural society, though inadequately revealed by our records, owned both land and *araghaṭṭas,* not in the form of a village community but as individual members of the village society. It is perhaps necessary to make this distinction somewhat clear. Although records may have referred to a community in the form of an ethnic or a caste group in association with a village such a reference need not necessarily define its total agrarian or social structure. It would simply point to the community affiliation of those who, in a context like the gift of rural produce, would essentially count only individually. At Saṁnānaka in 1176, the community mentioned was that of Gurjara cultivators[31] (a reference which is likely to recall the Gurjara cultivators of the Alwar region held by a segment of the Pratihāra lineage in the tenth century[32]), but when a grant was made, it was specified as having been made by Āśādhara, Siroiya and other *siras* or cultivators from a tract called Khadisira. At Sanderav, in 1164, a grant in the form of a grain share emanated from individual *rathakāras* like Dhanapāla, Surapāla, Jopāla, Sigada, Abhayapāla, Jisahada, Delhaṇa and others.[33] When in a different kind of context several *kuṭumbins* or cultivators of the village Nanana were displaced and made over (*pradatta*) to a temple establishment, they were enumerated individually by their personal names, and curiously, even at the moment when they were being deprived of their rights in the village, the designation indicating their status as cultivators (*kuṭumbin*) was retained.[34]

The several references cited above to individuals holding plots of land in the Godwad villages and making occasional gifts to temples may give the impression that the structure of a village was simply a juxtaposition of such a stratum of cultivator-proprietors and of those who secured various types of rights from the political system above the village in village land. No doubt such a stratum defined the core of the village society. The existence of a village-level organization, exercising certain rights in the conduct of village affairs is attested by the consent given by *mahājanas,* the *grāmīṇa* and the *janapada* when a document specifying levies for a temple was drawn up. On occasions, a *grāmapañcākula*[35] also figures in the context of decisions taken with regard to a village. However, the straturn of cultivators in association with other categories of village residents does not really stand in isolation from other social and political strata which, to return to the evidence provided by the village Koraṁṭaka, overlay the society at the village level. In Godwad, the nature of stratification within the layer of cultivator-proprietors cannot be worked out, but it is possible to an extent to work on another level, namely the nature of the linkage between the political system represented by the Nadol Cāhamāna kingdom and its rural settlements. An examination of this linkage can be undertaken from the perspective of how rural resources were distributed or transferred.

One way of examining this linkage—and we are making only a very tentative suggestion here—would be to identify the different nodes which either emerged from time to time or were stable supra-village points and with which individual villages were connected as a mechanism for channelizing village resources. The central point in the network of nodes was of course Nadol; it could at times even be the Caulukyan capital Aṇahilapura since Aṇahilapura, at moments when Caulukyan suzerainty extended to Nadol Cāhamāna territories, could restructure the distribution of superior rights in Nadol villages. But generally, the linkage between all individual rural settlements and such a central point may not have been so direct. Individual villages rather related more directly to several foci in the kingdom which could either be centres of urban dimensions or even be villages. In cases where a village itself was a node, the distinction with other villages arose because such a village was the *bhoga* of an important person in the kingdom (not always a member of the ruling lineage) or was a religions centre of importance. In fact, it could be both and it could be considered a node by virtue of its capacity to divert to itself the resources of other villages.

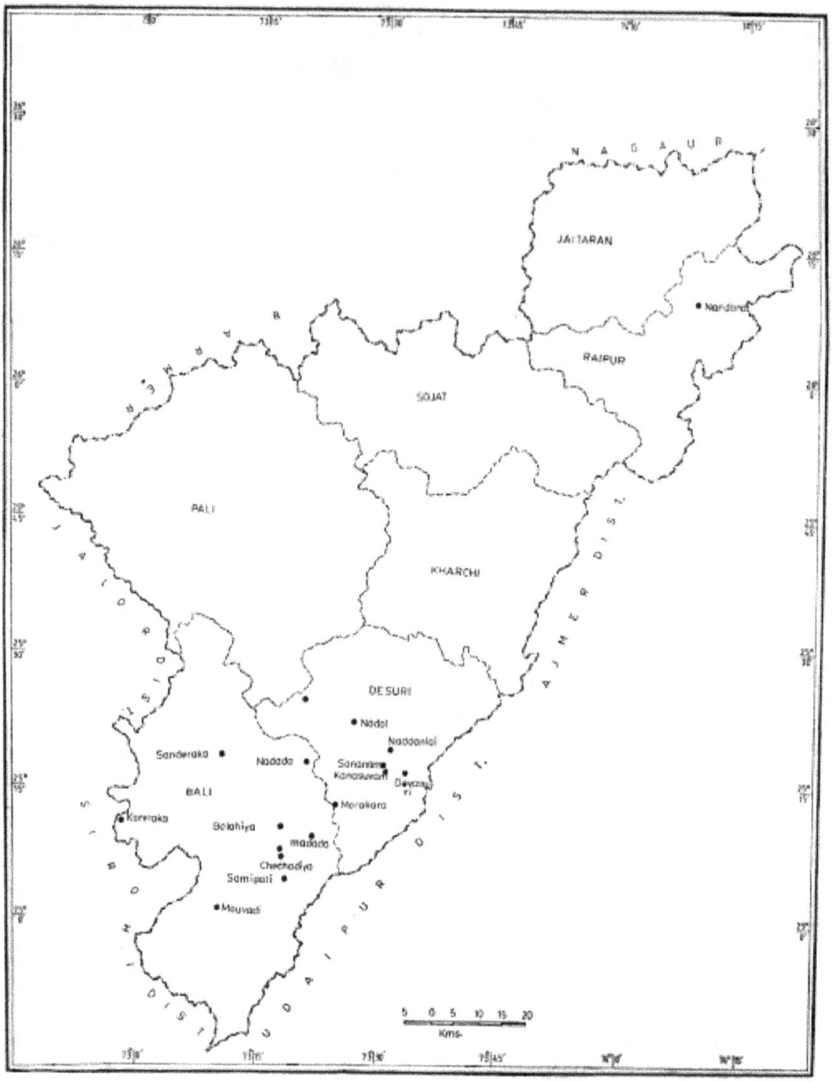

MAP 3.1: Some places mentioned in the records of Nadol-Cāhamānas (Pali district)

If the flow of resources from rural settlements to several points rather than to a single point in the Nadol Cāhamāna kingdom is accepted as a justification for assuming the existence of nodes, then the following may be thought of as such nodes: Samipāṭī, Bālahiya, Nāḍulaḍāgika or Naḍḍulāi, Ṣaṇḍeraka, Saṁnāṇaka and (Śrī) Naḍula.[36] Among these, Naḍḍulāi or Narlai and Naḍula or Nadol may be chosen, in view of the greater quantum of material relating to them, to illustrate the point being made. Several inscriptions of Narlai from the time of Rāyapāla

(1132 onward) refer to grants made at Narlai; they do not mention clearly whether contributions were received from villages outside Narlai, but an earlier inscription of 1130, recording a similar kind of gift, locates it in a village some distance away from Narlai.[37] It says that Cāhamāna Viṁsaraka, son of Pāpayara made a gift of a measure of oil from the *ghāṇaka* at Morakara to god Mahāvīra at Narlai. Morakara is identified with a village located about ten miles south-west of Narlai. By itself the evidence is of little value, but it assumes significance when taken in conjunction with another record, of 1160, from Nadol. The village Morakara figures in that year, in a list of twelve villages which together were officially attached to Naḍḍulāi and were given over as a favour to prince Kīrtipāla by king Ālhaṇa and *Yuvarāja* Kelhaṇa (*prasāde datta Naḍḍulāi-pratibaddha-dvādaśa-grāmāṇi*).[38] It is not that the arrangement was permanent, but even a temporary attachment of several villages, disparately located, to a central village, may perhaps to taken to bear out the idea of functional node.

Nadol as the centre of the kingdom, must have had a more extensive network; we focus here only on the network of its two deities; Tripuruṣadeva and Candaleśvara. They, along with other deities installed by members of the Nadol family, constituted what may be considered as the major cult complex of the kingdom.[39] It was royal patronage which linked the cult centre at Nadol with villages which were located some distance away from the centre. The deity Tripuruṣa enjoyed *Nandānā-grāma-bhoga* or the village of Nanana as a bhoga and the deity Candaleśvara the village of Bhimṭalavāḍa.[40] The incomes from these villages, expressed in such terms as *devakīyādāna* and *grāmādutpatti*, were distributed in the temple establishment in keeping with its ritual and other needs. For example, the *meharis* (or *devadāsis*) and instrumentalists of the temple received, from the incomes from these villages, grain shares which are specified in detail in Nanana records. However, Nanana and Bhiṁṭalavāḍa were not the only villages to which the control of the royal religious centre at Nadol extended, and the arrangements linking up such villages with the temple deities or other beneficiaries associated with the temple establishment were not immutable either. The village Devanaṁdita which was originally under the possession of the *maṭhapati* of Tripuruṣa was made over, along with its *araghaṭṭa* Nārāvaṭṭaka and two individuals, (Sila)pati and Śrīpāla,[41] at one stage to the deity Candaleśvara. A *devadāsi,* named Śobhikā, who till 1114 was receiving only five *droṇas* of grainshare from an *araghaṭṭa* at the village of Bhiṁṭalavāḍa, received a visit from the king Aśvarāja in that year and was awarded the income of the whole village of Pimcchavallī (*Pimcchavallī-grāma-sva-sīmā-paryanta*).[42] Since the village originally belonged to the *maṭha* of Candaleśvara, its transfer to a *devadāsi* in turn necessitated the gift of another village in its place to the *maṭha*. The village granted was Sālayī and the provisions of the gift were that two-third of its entire income (*sarvādāya*) would go to Candaleśvara and one-third to Tripuruṣa.[43] In 1163, the villages Nandānā and Bhiṁṭalavāḍa were restored to the possessions, respectively of Tripuruṣa and Candaleśvara, since these possessions had been disturbed for some time, and 3 *halas* of additional land, located on the 'western boundary of what is called Nījuṁhai-Duṁgara in the village Sāṁvoḍi' were added to the possessions of Tripuruṣa.[44]

Nadol's control over the villages from which state-patronized deities derived their income does not seem to have been limited to the simple act of transferring their resources. Apart from the fact that even such simple acts of transfer or resources could involve periodical readjustments, changes which could be of greater significance for the internal structure of the gift villages could assume several forms. The gift land could be given out on lease and this is precisely what is thought to have happened in the village of Bhiṁṭalavāḍa where, according to one document in a set of Nanana records, a lessee of an *araghaṭṭa* was requried to provide a fixed share out of its yield to a *devadāsi*.[45] The evidence is decidedly inadequate but the practice of leasing out a right which would yield a regular return was not uncommon in this period.[46] Second, this could tie up with another practice which occurs only in the context of villages which were transferred to the deities. An undated record of king Ratnapāla, in the same set of records from Nanana, contains the following expression: *Noriyākaḥ sa-kuṭumbaḥ pradattaḥ*; literally, it means: 'Noriyāka was given away along with relatives'.[47] The grantee was obviously either the deity Tripuruṣa or Candaleśvara, and the expression has been taken to mean that a certain individual named Noriyāka was made over to the deity along with his relatives. The purpose of the transfer of a number of individuals to a deity was not specified in the record; however, whatever its significance was, it was not an isolated case. Document number seven, dated 1135, of the Nanana records states that Kumāra Śrī Sāhanapāla gifted two cultivators (*kuṭumbikas*) Sohiya and Āsāica along with their sons and grandsons to the deity Tripuruṣadeva through a charter.[48] These *kuṭumbikas* were formerly residents of the village Nandānā which had become a *bhoga* of the deity. Several other *kuṭumbikas* of Nandānā-*grāma* and other individuals whose village affiliations are not specified were made over to the deity some years later in 1148 by king Ālhaṇa.[49] These gifts were made not only by the king or members of the royal family but by other individuals as well.[50]

What the transfer of individuals, including erstwhile cultivators, to the deity in a temple signifies, it is difficult to say. The evidence of the Nanana inscriptions is sometimes taken to suggest the prevalence of 'quasi-manorial' system in Marwar during the period of the Nadol Cāhamānas,[51] but the evidence occurs in too isolated a context to permit generalization of this kind. What seems to be significant is that most of the persons gifted away to the deity were originally residents and cultivators of the village which had come under the possession of the same deity. The displacement of the cultivators, their transfer to the deity and the possible introduction of the practice of leasing out land in the temple village thus, in some cases, could have been interconnected processes, ensuring flow of resources to Nadol where the deities were located.

A point of clarification is perhaps necessary at this stage. The nature of the linkage between what I have considered as nodes and villages related to them does not seem to have been uniform throughout the kingdom, and the nodes themselves do not seem to have remained fixed either. The reason for this may have been the regular need which arose for the redistribution of resources to new claimants, necessitating realignment of villages. This situation of flexible arrangements is in sharp contrast to the assurance normally accompanying a grant that it was in perpetuity. To cite once again the interesting case of *devadāsī* Śobhikā who caught the king's fancy and was rewarded with a village; the king's charter initially stipulated that no one should disturb her permanent possession of the village. However, the king does not appear to have been too sure, and the charter contained an additional provision that in the event of her losing the village, the *devadāsī* would receive back her annual grain share from the temple land in the village of Bhiṁṭalavāḍa:[52] Such shifts, when they actually took place, affected the link between the node and its villages. Two relevant cases may be cited. In 1143, when queen Tihunaka was enjoying the village Bālahiya, the various contributions raised for the festival of the local goddess Bahughṛṇā emanated from the same village and other villages related to it.[53] In 1159, Nadol was under the charge of a *daṇḍanāyaka* of the Caulukya king Kumarapāla, and grant to the same local goddess at Bālahiya emanated not from the village, which at that point of time was in the possession of a certain Anupameśvara, but from Nadol.[54] Apparently, in 1159, Bālahiya had ceased to function as a node. In 1160, Sonāṇā was one of twelve villages attached to Naḍḍulāi-*grāma* which was given over to *rājaputra* Kīrttipāla;[55] in 1176 Sonāṇā was both a *bhoga* of Kīrttipāla's sons and a node for villages, probably located in the area.[56]

III

The villages in the Nadol Cāhamāna kingdom—since they were sources of income for the members of the royal family and for those supported by them—were, thus, caught up in what were possibly inevitable shifts within the structure of Nadol Cāhamāna polity. The genealogical tables available for the Nadol Cāhamānas simply indicate almost linear progression from one rule to another,[57] without touching upon the complex problem of the structure of the lineage and its relationship with the pattern of the distribution of assignments or of distribution of resources from villages. When we remember that the core region of the Nadol Cāhamānas in this period corresponded to barely more than two tehsils (Bali and Desuri) in the Pali district, a probe into this relationship becomes crucial. For a somewhat clearer understanding of the linkage between the villages and the structure of Cāhamāna lineage, what is needed is to prepare a series of synchronic tables from which the composition of the royal and other assignees at given points of time could be ascertained. Our evidence is not adequate to prepare such synchronic views, but a restatement of certain details already cited but now relating to the periods of only two rulers, Aśvarāja and Kelhaṇa, may be made as a kind of substitute for synchronic tables.[58]

Inscriptions available for Aśvarāja range from 1110 to 1143. They refer to the victorious reign of Aśvarāja and to the *Yuvarāja* Kaṭukarāja, but the grants which they record did not emanate from the king alone. The Sevadi inscription of 1110 records gift of shares by a *mahāsāhaniya* from four villages which were obviously in his possession.[59] Samīpāṭī or Sevadi, described in another record in connection with a grant in cash as a *pattana,* was itself held by *Yuvarāja* Kaṭukarāja—in 1115.[60] In 1143, the village Bālahiya was the *grāsa* of the queen Tihuṇaka whose authority extended to other villages as well.[61] Around 1114, at least five villages figure in the Nanana records dealing with distribution of grain shares, grant of *araghaṭṭas a*nd of land to the deities Tripuruṣa and Candaleśvara and to individuals in the service of these deities.[62]

This pattern of distribution of land and resources to different categories of assignees, including those who were members of the royal family, was nothing uncommon, but what is uncommon is that Aśvarāja's period overlaps with other grants which did not have any reference to him. We have already cited the case of the village Morakarā, which in 1130 was held by a member of the Cāhamāna lineage unrelated to Aśvarāja[63] and was later incorporated in the rural territorial unit of which the centre was Naḍḍulāi.[64] In 1132, Naḍḍulāi was held by princes Rudrapāla and Amṛtapāla who along with their mother Mānaladevī made a grant to which all *grāmīṇakas,* merchants and other individuals acted as witnesses.[65] The ruler of this segment of the Nadol Cāhamāna lineage was Mahārājādhirāja Rāyapāladeva, and since his known years partly overlap with those of Aśvarāja, it could be assumed that the Nadol Cāhamāna kingdom consisted of distinct territorial segments (with centres at Nadol and Naḍḍulāi) within which distribution of rural settlements or resources from them among different categories of assignees was organized. However, such a clearcut distinction would be ultimately found unsatisfactory for, in 1135, well within the period of Aśvarāja, we find Rāyapāla's son Ṣāhanapāla or Sahajapāla making grants to Tripuruṣa—the deity with which Aśvarāja was closely associated.[66] Second, empirical evidence also suggests that assigned villages did not correspond to a fixed segment. As we have seen, in 1132, Naḍḍulāi was in the possession of the princes Rudrapāla and Amṛtapāla, but even during the reign of their father Rāyapāla, it passed on to Guhila *rāuta ṭhakkura* Rājadeva, son of *rāuta ṭhakkura* Udharaṇa. Rājadeva was the *bhokṭāri* of Naḍḍulāi roughly from 1138 to 1145 and is known from several Naḍḍulāi records to have made donations from various sources of his income.[67] In 1160, a further change took place when twelve villages were attached to Naḍḍulāi and assigned to prince Kīrtipāla, who belonged to the segment represented by Aśvarāja. The records of the period of Kelhaṇa, the last ruler we discuss, range from 1163 and 1179, and reveal further shifts in the history of Naḍḍulāi. Since *Rājaputra* Kīrttipāla, *bhoktā* of Naḍḍulāi group of villages in 1160, figures in an official capacity in a record from Bamnera in 1163, one may perhaps presume that he still held Naḍḍulāi in that year.[68] In 1171, however, Sonāṇā, one of Naḍḍulāi villages, was under *ṭhakkura* Anasīha,[69] but by 1176 had passed on to princes Lāṣanapāla and Abhayapāla,[70] suggesting further segmentation of what may be called the *bhoga* of Naḍḍulāi.

We do not know what kind of pressure within and outside the Nadol Cāhamāna lineage may have led to the expansion of the domain of the Nadol Cāhamānas into Jalor, Sirohi, Mandor and other areas soon after.[71] The fact that *bhoga, grāsa* or *sejā* rights often changed hands would suggest the existence of some kind of pressure; to this were added other sources of pressure: outside the ruling lineage were other

Rajput lineages, such as the Guhila, Cāhamāna and Rāṣṭrakūṭa who too shared rights in land along with two common categories of assignees, the brāhmaṇas and the temples. What emerges as relevant from all this for our discussion is that the Nadol Cāhamāna records do not permit us to view the rural settlements of the Nadol region individually or in isolation but only with reference to certain key points within the kingdom. These points were what integrated the rural bases of the kingdom, and by representing these points, the various categories of the *bhoktās* or assignees indicate, on the one hand, the nature of the linkage between rural settlements and those who held superior rights over them and, on the other, between such right-holders and the Nadol Cāhamāna kingdom.

NOTES

1. The Godwad division was part of the old Jodhpur State.
2. For description of Godwad see K.K. Sehgal, *Rajasthan District Gazetteers: Pali* (Directorate of District Gazetteers, Government of Rajasthan, Jaipur, 1976). See also *Progress Report of the Archaeological Survey of India: Western Circle,* 1908, p. 48.
3. For a narrative account of Nadol Cāhamāna history, prepared from the perspective of dynastic history, see Dasarath Sharma, *Early Chauhan Dynasties: A Study of Chauhan Political History, Chauhan Political Institutions and Life in the Chauhan Dominions from c.800* to *1316 AD,* Delhi, 1959, Chaps. 12-16.
4. For sources on legends around the adventures of Lakṣmaṇa, ibid., Chap. 12.
5. F. Kielhorn, 'The Chahamanas of Naḍḍula', *EI,* vol. 9, Calcutta, 1907-8, p. 83.
6. See Chapter 1 of this volume.
7. For example, the Jalor stone inscription of Samarasiṁha (*Vikrama Samvat* 1239) refers to subjugation of the *taskaras* of the entire region of Pīlvāhikā. Keeping in view the expressions used with reference to tribes by the ruling lineages of the period, D.R. Bhandarkar correctly takes *taskara* to mean the 'unsettled tribes' of the region, D.R. Bhandarkar, 'The Chahamanas of Marwar', *EI,* vol. 11, no. 18, Calcutta, 1911-12, pp. 26-79.
8. Ram Karna, 'Bijapur Inscription of Dhavala of Hastikundi', *EI,* vol. 10, Calcutta, 1909-10, pp. 17-24.
9. See B.D. Chattopadhyaya, 'Markets and Merchants in early medieval Rajasthan', *The Making of Early Medieval India,* 2nd edn., Delhi, 2012, pp. 93–123.
10. *Progress Report of the Archaeological Survey of India: Western Circle: year ending 1909*, p. 44 ff; also Sharma, *Early Chauhan Dynasties,* p. 138.

11. See inscriptions of the Nadol Cāhamānas, ed. F. Kielhorn, op. cit., and Bhandarkar, op. cit.
12. Bhandarkar, op. cit., pp. 43-5.
13. For example, Bali stone inscription of Āśvāka of *vikrama samvat* 1200; Bhandarkar, op. cit., pp. 32-3. Also Kiradu stone inscription of Ālhaṇadeva, *vikrama samvat* 1209, ibid., pp. 43-4.
14. The crucial importance of wells for irrigation and, therefore, for the emergence of rural settlements in the region is evident from the semi-arid conditions of the region in which neither the major river Luni nor its affluents such as Jawai or Sukri can provide water for irrigation. The region's precipitation level being low and rate of evaporation being high, surface storage is totally inadequate. These conditions underline the importance of the utilization of groundwater reserves. For geographical features of the region see Sehgal, *Rajasthan District Gazetteers: Pali;* V.C. Misra, *Geography of Rajasthan,* Delhi, 1967, chaps. 4, 5 and 11; K.D. Erskine, *Imperial Gazetteer of India: Provincial Series* (*Rajputana*), Calcutta, 1908, pp. 48-9, 172-3. According to a recent account, the village Kotri, located near the river Sukri in Desuri tehsil, has 40 wells, used for irrigation, dotted over the village area, R.L. Singh, ed., *India: A Regional Geography* (National Geographical Society of India, Varanasi, repr. 1987), p. 64.

    Of the 8 bedrock formations in Western Rajasthan listed by G.C. Taylor, it seems that groundwater as source for irrigation in the region was tapped from Aravalli slates and Malani volcanic series; see G.C. Taylor, 'The Occurrence of groundwater in rocks of western Rajasthan', *Proceedings of the Symposium on the Rajputana Desert* (*Bulletin of the National Institute of Sciences of India*), no. 1, 1952, pp. 217-21.
15. Bhandarkar, 'The Chahamanas of Marwar', pp. 29-30.
16. Ibid., pp. 32-3.
17. Ibid., pp. 49-50.
18. Note 16.
19. Note 17; also ibid., pp. 50-1.
20. The variants of *ḍhiku* are *ḍhikuau, ḍhikaḥ, ḍhiṁvaḍau* and *ḍhiṁkaḥ;* see M.B. Gadre, 'Three Copperplate Grants of the Time of the Chahamana Kelhaṇa', *EI,* vol. 13, Calcutta, 1915-16, pp. 206-11.
21. Ibid.
22. *Progress Report of the Archaeological Survey of India, Western Circle, Year Ending 1917,* p. 65.
23. The difference between *ḍhiku* and *araghaṭṭa* is not clear even in *Rajasthani Sabad Kosh,* ed. S.R. Lalas, vol. 2, pt. I, s.v. *ḍhimadau.* However, *ḍhiku* seems to correspond to *dhenkli* used in shallow wells. It 'consists of a stout rod, balanced on a vertical post, and having a heavy weight at one end and a leather bucket or earthen pot suspended by a rope to the other. The worker dips the bucket or pot into the water, and aided by the counterpoising weight, empties it into a hole from which a channel

conducts the water to the lands to be irrigated. Water is sometimes lifted from streams in the same way'; K.D. Erskine, *Imperial Gazetteer,* p. 49.

24. For *araghaṭṭas* see B.D. Chattopadhyaya, 'Irrigation in Early Medieval Rajasthan', in *The Making of Early Medieval India*, pp. 38–58.
25. Gadre, 'Three Copperplate Grants of the Time of the Chahamana Kelhana.'
26. For the meaning of *ḍohalikā* as non-transferable landgrant to brahmins, *caraṇas,* or religious/charitable institutions see Gadre, 'Three Copperplate Grants of the Time of the Chahamana Kelhana' and Erskine, Imperial Gazetteer, pp. 188-9.
27. Bamnera record no. B of Vikrama Samvat 1223, Gadre, 'Three Copperplate Grants of the Time of the Chahamana Kelhana.'
28. The location of both Bamnera where the plates were found and of Korta, identified with the place mentioned in the plates, near Erinpura railway station suggests this identification.
29. The *grāma* of Koraṁṭaka or Koretaka has been described in Bamnera plate B as *rājaputra Ajayarājakīya-sejā;* Gadre, 'Three Copperplate Grants of the Time of the Chahamana Kelhana.'
30. The inscription records a grant by Śrīmahārājādhirāja Śrī Rāyapāladeva in the presence of the *mahājanas, grāmīṇas* and *janapada*; Bhandarkar, 'The Chahamanas of Marwar', pp. 41–2.
31. Lalrai stone inscription of Lākhanapāla and Abhayapāla, Vikrama Samvat 1233; ibid., pp. 50–1.
32. F. Kielhorn, 'Rajor Inscription of Mathanadeva, (Vikrama) Samvat 1016', *EI,* vol. 3, Calcutta, 1894-5, p. 266, line 12.
33. Sanderav stone inscription of Kelhaṇadeva, Vikrama Samvat 1221; Bhandarkar, 'The Chahamanas of Marmar', pp. 46–7.
34. D.C. Sircar, 'Stray plates from Nanana', *EI,* vol. 33, Delhi, 1960, pp. 238–46.
35. Lalrai stone inscription of Kelhaṇadeva, Vikrama Samvat 1233; Bhandarkar, pp. 49–50.
36. See the map showing locations of identifiable places in the Nadol Cāhamāna kingdom.
37. *Progress Report of the Archaeological Survey of India, Western Circle, year ending 1909,* p. 41 ff.
38. Nadol Plates of Rājaputra Kīrtipāla, Vikrama Samvat 1218; F. Kielhorn, 'The Cāhamānas of Naḍḍula', pp. 66-70. The list of villages and their suggested identifications are as follows: Naddūlāigrāma (Narlai), Sūjera (Sujapura), Harijī (Harji), Kavīlāḍam (Kailvada), Sonāṇam (Sonana), Morakarā (Morkha), Haravaṁdam, Māḍāḍā (Modada or Mundada), Kāṇasuvam (Kana), Devasuri (Desuri), Nāḍāḍā (Nadana), Mauvaḍī (Mori or Modi). For suggested identifications see Ram Karna, 'Nadol plates of the Maharajputra Kīrtipāla of Vikrama Samvat 1218', *The Indian Antiquary,* vol. 40, 1911, pp. 144–6.
39. The royal cult centre of which Tripuruṣa was the chief deity would require a separate study. However, the practice of the installation of

deities named after members of the Nadol Cāhamāna lineage and the nature of royal patronage extended to the centre, as provided in detail in the Nanana plates, point to the existence of a royal cult complex. Some of the deities mentioned in the records may be listed to highlight the point: Lakṣmaṇasvāmī (probably named after the founder of the family), *EI*, vol. 11, pp. 26-8, Padmaleśvara (named after Padmalladevī, queen of Rāyapāla), Ṣāhanapaleśvara (named after Ṣāhanapāla), Sahajapāleśvara (named after Sahajapāla), Caṁdaleśvara (named after Candaladevī), etc.; Sircar, 'Stray Plates from Nanana'.

40. These and other details that follow are from the Nanana plates; Sircar, 'Stray plates from Nanana'.
41. Ibid., p. 241.
42. Ibid., p. 242.
43. Ibid.
44. S. Sankaranarayanan, 'Nanana copperplates of the time of Kumārapāla and Ālhaṇa, Vikrama Samvat 1212 and 1220', *EI*, vol. 39, pt. I, Delhi, 1981, pp. 17-26.
45. D.C. Sircar, 'Stray Plates from Nanana'.
46. See Chattopadhyaya, 'Markets and Merchants'.
47. Sircar, 'Stray Plates from Nanana'.
48. Ibid.
49. Ibid.
50. Ibid.
51. L. Gopal, 'Quasi-manorial rights in ancient India', *Journal of the Economic and Social History of the Orient*, vol. 6, 1963, pp. 296-308.
52. Sircar, 'Stray Plates from Nanana'.
53. Bali Stone Inscription of Āśvāka, *Vikrama Samvat* 1200; Bhandarkar, 'The Chahamanas of Marwar', pp. 32-3.
54. *Progress Report of the Archaeological Survey of India, Western Circle, year ending 1908*, p. 55.
55. Kielhorn, 'Rajor Inscription of Mathanadeva, (Vikrama) Samvat 1016', pp. 68-70.
56. See Nadlai stone inscription of Kelhaṇa, Vikrama Samvat 1228; Lalrai Stone inscription of Kelhaṇadeva, Vikrama Samvat 1233; Lalrai stone inscription of Lākhanapāla and Abhayapāla, Vikrama Samvat 1233; Bhandarkar, 'The Chahamanas of Marnear', pp. 47-51.
57. See the genealogical table in Dasaratha Sharma, *Early Chauhan Dynasties*, p. 332.
58. See also Appendix 1 of this volume.
59. Bhandarkar, 'The Chahamanas of Marwar', pp. 28-9.
60. Ibid., pp. 30-2.
61. Ibid., pp. 32-3.
62. Sircar, 'Stray Plates from Nanana'.
63. *Progress Report of the Archaeological Survey of India,. Western Circle, year ending 1909*, p. 41 ff.

64. Kielhorn, 'Rajor Inscription of Mathanadeva, (Vikrama) Samvat 1016', pp. 68-70.
65. Nadlai stone inscription of Rāyapāla, Vikrama Samvat 1189; D.R. Bhandarkar, op. cit., pp. 34-6.
66. Sircar, 'Stray Plates from Nanana'.
67. Nadlai stone inscription of Rāyapāla, Vikrama Samvat 1195; Nadlai stone inscription of Rāyapāla, Vikrama Samvat 1200; Nadlai stone inscription of Rāyapāladeva, Vikrama Samvat 1202; Bhandarkar, 'The Chahamanas of Marwar', pp. 37-43.
68. Gadre, 'Three Copperplate Grants'.
69. Nadlai stone inscription of Kelhaṇa, Vikrama Samvat 1228; Bhandarkar, 'The Chahamanas of Marwar', pp. 47-8.
70. Ibid., pp. 49-50.
71. For chronology of the movement of the Nadol Cāhamānas into these areas see Sharma, *Early Chauhan Dynasties*.

Appendix 1

Assignments and Assignees in Nadol Cāhamāna Kingdom: Epigraphic References

(References to assignments are not always direct but have sometimes to be made out from the nature of an individual's or a group of individuals' association with a place)

Date	*Assignment and the term used*	*Assignee*	*Reference*
1110	Padrāḍā*grāma* Medraṁcā*grāma* Chechaḍiyāmad-daḍī-*grāma*	Mahāsāhanīya Uppālaraka, during the reign of Aśvarāja	*EI,* 11, pp. 28-30
1114? 1162	Nandāṇāgrāmakīya-*bhoga*	Deity Tripuruṣa	*EI,* 33, pp. 240-3 *EI,* 39, pp. 17-26
1162	3 *halas* of land in Saṁvoḍi village	Deity Tripuruṣa	Ibid.
1114? 1162	Bhiṁṭalavāḍa-*grāma*	Deity Candaleśvara	Ibid.
1114	Piñchavalli-*grāma*	*Mehari* Śobhikā, during the reign of Aśvarāja	*EI,* 33, pp. 240-3
1114	Sālayī-*grāma*	*Maṭha* of Tripuruṣa, during the reign of Aśvarāja	Ibid.
1115	*Bhukti* of Samipāṭī-pattana	Kaṭukarāja, son of Aśvarāja	*EI,* 11, pp. 30-2
1138 1143 1145	Naduladāgika	Guhila *bhoktātri ṭhakkura* Rājadeva	*EI,* 11, pp. 36-7, 41-3

(*Contd.*)

1143	Bālahiya-*grāma* enjoyed as *grāsa*	Queen Tihuṇaka, during the reign of Aśvarāja	*EI,* 11, pp. 32-3
1143	Samīpāṭī	Yuvarāja Jayatasīha, during the reign of Kaṭukadeva	*EI,* 11, pp. 33-4
1159	Bālahi (ya)	Anupameśvara, subordinate of Vayajaladeva, *daṇḍanāyaka* of Caulukya Kumārapāla	*PRASWC,* 1908, p. 55
1159	*Hala* of land at Balahi	Deity Bahughṛṇā	Ibid.
1160	Naddulāi-*grāma* along with 12 villages given as *prasāda*	Rājaputra Kīrttipāla, during the reign of Kelhaṇa	*EI,* 9, pp. 66-70
1163 1164	Koraṁṭaka	*Sejā* of *rājaputra* Ajayasīha, during the reign of Ālhaṇa	*EI,* 13, pp. 207-11
1163 1164	*Ḍohalika* at Koraṁṭaka and other grants	Brāhmaṇa Nārāyaṇa	Ibid.
1164	*Rājakīya-bhoga* of Ṣaṇḍeraka	Queenmother Ānaladevī	*EI,* 11, pp. 46-7
1171	Boripadyaka	Rāṇā Lakhāmaṇarāja	*EI,* 11, p. 48
1171	Sonāṇā*grāma*	*Ṭhakkura* Anasīhu	Ibid.
1176	*Bhukti* of Sinānava of Saṁnāṇaka	Rājaputra Lāṣaṇapāla, rājaputra Abhayapāla and queen Mahībaladevī	*EI,* 11, pp. 49-50
1179	*Bhukti* of Ṣaṇḍeraka	Queen Jālhaṇadevī	*EI,* 11, pp. 51-2.

Four

Kalikaṭṭi: An Early Medieval Village in South Karnataka

THIS ESSAY MAKES an attempt to prepare a sketch of the chronological history of a single—but perhaps in many ways an important—early medieval village in south Karnataka. The village was consistently referred to as Kalikaṭṭi in its epigraphic records which cover a span of about hundred years. There are certain points which appear to be of significance about the village as a theme of study. It has yielded twelve inscriptions,[1] in addition to three more from other villages which refer to it. For a period for which source material on rural settlements is generally available in the form of mere reference to the name of a village, this relative richness of epigraphic material would appear to be rather unusual. With the exception of one record found outside Kalikaṭṭi, all other epigraphs relate to the period of the Hoysaḷa rulers of south Karnataka. Second, although Kalikaṭṭi, identifiable with Kanakatte in the Arsikere taluk of Hassan district,[2] lay in what may be called the nuclear region of the Hoysaḷas, Kalikaṭṭi had its distinct identity as a village with a composite society and not merely as an integral administrative unit of the Hoysaḷa domain.[3] This is not to say that Kalikaṭṭi lay outside the sphere of royal influence or intervention. It was too close to the Hoysaḷa capital to escape intervention. The

* This essay could not have been written without the help that I was able to receive from Sri Ashok Shettar, Lecturer in the Department of History and Archaeology, Karnatak University, Dharwad. Sri Shettar selected the inscriptions which constitute the material for this essay, patiently read through them over and over again with me, not only pointed out inadequacies in Rice's translations but also verbally translated all of them and provided comments on difficult expressions. If my 'reconstruction' is different from what he expected it to be, it is perhaps because no two individuals' perceptions of what is more relevant can be identical.

Kalikaṭṭi records—which originate in the village itself and are not in the nature of copperplate charters drawn up elsewhere—nevertheless give the impression that Hoysaḷa royal measures with regard to the village were responses to what was happening in the village at different points of time. There were, thus, several stages of intervention, which lead on to the third point which is that the inscriptional records of Kalikaṭṭi, though unevenly spread over about hundred years during the Hoysaḷa rule and at times, impossible to get satisfactory meanings out of, nevertheless present an impression of changes in their contents. These changes may legitimately be taken to bear upon what was happening at the level of the village society, and if no other worthwhile generalization regarding early medieval rural settlements emerges from this study, the Kalikaṭṭi evidence should at least be a pointer to the possibility of certain kinds of change that could and did take place at the level of the village society in early medieval India.

The earliest reference to Kalikaṭṭi is pre-Hoysaḷa. A herostone inscription of *c.*AD 890 from Arakere (also in Arsikere taluk),[4] dated to the time of Gaṅga Satyavākya Permānadi Rācamalla, described in the record as the ruler of the earth, and of his nephew Erayapparasa, described as ruling the whole kingdom, records the death on battlefield *Sāmanta* Śrī Muttara, governor of *Āsandi-nāḍu. Sāmanta Śrī* Muttara who belonged to Bali-*Vaṁśa* fell fighting against the Nolambas, but his death earned him a posthumous *vṛtti* (*kal-nāḍu*) consisting of Arikere and Kalikaṭṭi. The herostone is found at Arakere, identifiable with Arikere of the inscription, and it would seem that of the two villages constituting the *Vṛtti* (*Kal-nāḍu*) Arikere was the more important—at least in *c.*890.

When Kalikaṭṭi is mentioned again—after a lapse of about two hundred and forty years—it was the first village (*modalavāḍa*) of Magare 300 :[5] the foremost village in a designated territorial unit, the kinds of which are mentioned in the records of the Deccan as also elsewhere.[6] What led to the transformation of Kalikaṭṭi into the foremost village of Magare 300 division we do not know, but the earliest Hoysaḷa period records from the village, belonging to the time of king Viṣṇuvardhana, (1108-42) present certain features which may be considered to have been associated with the process of stabilizing the linkage between the village and the now independent Hoysaḷa kingdom. The earliest inscription, dated 1130, speaks of one *Mahāsāmanta* Siṅgarasa of Arasikere who obtained Kalikaṭṭi free from all obstructions (*sarvva-vādhā-pariharam*) and governed it (*āluttam*).[7] Siṅgarasa installed a deity Siṅgeśvara, obviously named after him, and made certain grants to the

Kālāmukha priest Kriyāśaktipaṇḍita for providing certain services to the temple.[8] The grants consisted of two types of land; dry land (*beḷdale*) located to the south of the temple and wet land (*gardde*) located in an open space of the first ridge of the small sluice of the big tank (*hiriya-kere*) of the village. The inscription provides a genealogy of Siṅgarasa who is also mentioned as a ruler of Kunigilu-*naḍ* and as one born to be a 'ruler of 800'. The interesting feature of the genealogy is that at least two predecessors of Siṅgarasa are described as 'pledged warriors' (*Kurālu* or *Kaṭṭāḷu*) and another one had the appellation Nolamba-*gāvuṇḍa*, suggesting affiliation with the Nolambas. The background of Siṅgarasa, governing Kalikaṭṭi at the early stage of Hoysaḷa independent rule, thus, appears to have been that of a professional warrior group, probably originally owing allegiance to the Nolambas.[9] In fact, although Siṅgarasa refers to himself as *tatpādapadmopajīvin* (subsisting on his lotus feet) in relation to Viṣṇuvardhana, the inscription at the same time describes him as *samadhigata-pañcamahāśabda-Nolamba-deva-pād-ārādhaka* (i.e. worshipper of the feet of Nolambadeva). The second record, of 1132,[10] of *Mahāsāmanta* Siṅgarasa curiously refers to him as having been removed from Arasikere (literally, 'lifted from Arasikere'), the centre from which he was ruling Kalikaṭṭi, and brought to Kalikaṭṭi which he continued to govern. In 1132 Siṅgarasa, in the presence of all people in the village (*samastaprajā-galu*) installed another deity, a *liṅga* called Beṭṭadakalideva (Kalideva of the hills), believed to be a deity of the warriors. He made grants for this deity too, through a Śaiva priest Sekarajiya, grandson of Beṭṭadajiya. The grants consisted of dry fields and wet fields located in different areas, and once again the point of reference for the location of the wet fields was the big tank of the village. Siṅgarasa, thus, seems to have been as involved in the affairs of the village in 1132 as he was before his removal from Arasikere. Why he was removed is not known. That this was an event of some significance is suggested by the fact that it was mentioned once again in a later inscription, of the period of Ballāla II.[11] Could it be that because of his background the newly established Hoysaḷa state was keen to contract his spheres of authority and make sure that he operated from a single village base, however prosperous that village may already have become?

It is not my intention to summarize, in a chronological order, the contents of the Hoysaḷa period inscriptions from Kalikaṭṭi. I did so with the earliest two records of the period to present the nature of the evidence with regard to the status of Kalikaṭṭi as a rural settlement in the core area of the Hoysaḷa state at this stage. In trying to study the characteristics of Kalikaṭṭi, or for that matter of any other early medieval village as a rural settlement, all one can do is to depend entirely on incidental references. As elsewhere, the records are mostly of religious association, concerned with what were considered to be important social acts like the installation of deities and construction of temples and with various categories of grants made to them to keep certain types of services (*aṅgabhoga, raṅgabhoga, naivedya, atithi-abhyāgatāhāra* and so on) in operation. The grants, however, incidentally, do refer to the agricultural landscape of the village (although a satisfactory reconstruction of the total landscape from these scraps of information is impossible) and to the groups which were drawn into the social activities centring round the temples, either already in existence or newly created. An inscription of 1189, of the time of Ballāla II,[12] describes Kalikaṭṭi as an agrarian settlement in glowing terms: 'With wellfilled beautiful tanks, with areca plams, with fields of *gandhaśāli* rice such as caused Lakṣmī of forests to open her eyes and with fine temples Kalikaṭṭi shone among notable settlements'. Eulogies of Kalikaṭṭi, substantially similar, occur in other records. The settlement term used here is *ur* which, to use Coḷa period evidence from Tamilnadu, was a non-brahmadeya rural settlement.[13] The settlement designations for Kalikaṭṭi were really rather varied, but I shall come to that point later. The description of Kalikaṭṭi presented in the inscription which I have cited was not unique; this was what an ideal rural settlement, whether of the *brahmadeya-agrahāra* or *ur* variety, was supposed to have been like.[14] Yet, whatever partial glimpses the records offer of the agrarian landscape of Kalikaṭṭi lend some credence to the eulogy. I have already referred to an important landmark of the village, i.e. the big tank (*hiriya-kere*) which must have come into existence before the Hoysaḷa period. The exact location of the tank in the village is nowhere indicated; nor do we know its exact capacity to irrigate. In fact the irrigation capacities of the numerous tanks or reservoirs built in the early medieval period—some of them apparently so big as to be called *samudram*—are never a part of the eulogistic references made about them; estimates, as yet largely uncorroborated, with regard to some early medieval tanks which are still in use have only recently been made.[15] For Kalikaṭṭi, the big tank remained the big tank even when new tanks were constructed, or natural water formations were transformed into reservoirs. Of the twelve inscriptions at Kalikaṭṭi, seven refer to the big tank[16] and, incidentally, to some of its sections. Three inscriptions, of 1130, 1143 and 1153, mention the first ridge of its small sluice (*cikka-tumbu*); another inscription, of 1132, refers to its stone sluice.[17] The references are all, except in one case, to wet lands (*gardde*).[18] It was possible to bring new land in the area of the big tank under cultivation, as suggested by the location of certain gift lands in the open space (*bayalu*) close to the sluice of the big tank.[19] Such land was located near other tanks as well. We know nothing regarding the ownership of the big tank or how exactly its water was distributed; what appears to be of some significance is that grants of wet land and dry land near the tank, of which the temples were in variably the beneficiaries, emanated either from the rulers of the village or were made with the approval of the Hoysaḷa king.[20] Another tank, Āḍuva-*gere*, mentioned in the context of both wet and dry land distribution, appears in the records of the early phase of Hoysaḷa rule in Kalikaṭṭi and in the order of gifts recorded may be listed next to the donations made near the big tank.[21] The donations recorded in an epigraph of 1143 consisted of one *Khaṇḍuga* of wet land, in the open space (*bayalu*) of the first ridge of the big sluice (*hiriya-tumbu*) of Āḍuva-*gere* given by *Sāmanta* Goyideva, ruler of the village,[22] and of the same measure of wet land in the same location given by Sataya-*nāyaka*, grandson of Hoysaḷa-*gāvuṇḍa* of Kalikaṭṭi.[23] A further gift, of a stretch of dry land, specified as the inner land of Āḍuva-*gere,* is recorded in the same epigraph.[24]

The big tank (*hiriya-kere*) and Āḍuva-*gere* may not have been privately owned but there were other tanks in Kalikaṭṭi which were. An inscription of 1132 records the gift of two plots of dry land to a newly installed deity Beṭṭadakalideva, one of which was located behind Hariyoja's tank.[25] Hariyoja, to judge from the *Yoja* suffix in his name, obviously belonged to the community of artisans in the village, and was owner of the tank mentioned as his tank. Another tank, apparently privately owned, was Maṅgeya's tank mentioned in three records, of 1208, 1209 and 1211.[26] Gift lands specified in these records are mentioned as lying under Maṅgeya's tank, but since the purpose of these inscriptions was to record constructions of new tanks and also creation of the nucleus of a new settlement, it may be presumed that the donated lands were not irrigated by Maṅgeya's tank, and that the references to it were references to an existing landmark in the village. One more private tank was Boviti's tank, perhaps a tank owned by the wife of a Bova—a member of a community often mentioned in the Kalikaṭṭi records—which was located behind the Biṭṭeya-*samudra* (i.e. Biṭṭeya's tank), newly constructed in 1208-9.[27]

Some tanks were in existence at the beginning of Hoysaḷa rule, others were constructed later. In fact, the inscriptions reveal that minor as well as major initiatives were taken either to better utilize existing sources of water for irrigation or to create new ones, both resulting in an expansion of the agrarian space of the village. Relevant evidence is available both from Kalikaṭṭi and from its periphery. A Kalikaṭṭi inscription of 1143 lists one *mattar* of dry land, located along a channel (*bayikalu*) among gifts made to the temple of the deity Kaligeśvara installed by a brāhmaṇa Āḷvi Bhaṭṭa.[28] Taking advantage of the existence of a natural accumulation of water (*nirugal*), Āḷvi Bhaṭṭa spent some cash (*honnu*, literally meaning gold), set up a sluice to the east of the temple and converted the dry land into *melumakki* (a category of wet land), yielding good rice. Other such channels and streams were also obviously used for purposes of irrigation. An inscription of the time of Ballāla II which records donation of land by queen Umādevī specifies the gift as three *salages* of wet land located to the east of a stream (*halla*).[29] Another record, of 1152,[30] seems to refer to a different natural accumulation of water (*nirugaṭṭa*), near the first ridge of which were donated two *mattars* of dry land to the deity Jagateśvara by Mahāpradhāna Senādhipati Hiriya-heggaḍe Ballanna, the governor of Kalikaṭṭi. The same water formation is described in clear terms as a tank (*Kere*) in an inscription of the time of Ballāla II;[31] the context in which it was described as a tank was the donation of three *salages* of wet land near its western section.

Kalikaṭṭi, the first village of Magare 300, was called along with its hamlets (*halli, hiriyur*), in the records of the early thirteenth century, Kalikaṭṭi *sthala*.[32] It was also called a *nāḍ*.[33] Clearly, the agrarian space of Kalikaṭṭi was expanding. An inscription (*c*.1215), by way of giving certain details regarding reallocation of temple funds, clearly suggests that *hallis* or hamlets were components of a settlement structure that had come to be perceived as Kalikaṭṭi-*sthala*.[34] One such *halli* was Biṭṭena-*halli*, the establishment of which may be traced, around 1208-9,[35] to Heḍeya or Hoḍeya Biṭṭeya. The establishment of Biṭṭena-*halli* was marked by the construction of two new tanks and installation of two new deities.[36] The *halli* was the nucleus of a new settlement, located away from Kalikaṭṭi, but it was a *halli* of Kalikaṭṭi; some of the wet land, dry land and garden land donated by Hoḍeya Biṭṭeya to the newly installed deities appear to have been located in Kalikaṭṭi, the location of the garden land being near the important landmark of the village, i.e. the *hiriya-kere* or the big tank.[37]

By putting together isolated scraps of information regarding the existence of old tanks, construction of new tanks or the use of water from various other sources, I am not, I must hasten to add, arguing that hydraulic arrangements were the lynchpin around which all economic and social activity at Kalikaṭṭi revolved. However, the inscriptions, by repeatedly referring to them in the context of the location of donated land as also in the context of the emergence of new nuclei of settlement, identify them as landmarks in Kalikaṭṭi's agrarian landscape. It appears from the records that they, along with the temples of the village in some cases, were the natural points of reference whenever distribution or transfer of village land had to be undertaken by different categories of donors from within or outside the village, much in the same way as *nadī, gaṅginikā, srota,* etc., were, in similar contexts, natural points of reference in Bengal and *araghaṭṭa*-wells in western Rajasthan.

II

If expansion of agrarian space represents one dimension of change in Kalikaṭṭi, another facet of change may be brought into focus by examining the nature of external political authority over the village. Before I take up whatever evidence is available regarding the social groups living in Kalikaṭṭi, I would like to examine this aspect of Kalikaṭṭi's history. This priority is suggested by the inscriptions themselves. Although Kalikaṭṭi was not a self-governing village 'republic', it will be difficult, given the nature of the data, to prepare a narrative history of how it was ruled during the Hoysaḷa period. In fact, it seems, even from the profusion of non-political details of the epigraphs, that there were points of break in the history of Kalikaṭṭi, and it may be possible to mark these points if we pursue its history up to the stage to which it appears intelligible and regular.

I have already mentioned that toward the close of the ninth century Kalikaṭṭi was, along with another village, given away as a posthumous *vṛtti,* but by the time the village was heard of again, some two hundred and forty years later, it was not being held as *vṛtti* by any particular family of rulers. Yet we find, from the time of Viṣṇuvardhana, a succession of rulers of subordinate status claiming that they were governing Kalikaṭṭi, after having obtained it free from all impediments. Did this phenomenon lead to the emergence of a permanent base of *Sāmanta* or feudatory control in the village? Kalikaṭṭi's inscriptions answer this question with a firm negative; as will be seen later, after a certain, stage in its history, records emanating from these governors seem to cease. Who then were the governors and what was the nature of their involvement in the village?

Two points may be made at this stage, before we attempt to respond to these questions. First, Kalikaṭṭi had ceased to be a *vṛtti* and, at the same time, it was not a base of power of a local chief. This should not mean that at the time that Hoysaḷa Viṣṇuvardhana was still consolidating his power, it had, as a *ur* village, an undifferentiated village community. Second, at least in the early stage of its history, there is no evidence of the existence of a substantial brāhmaṇa group in the village. Deities, and temples in which they were enshrined, constituted at this stage the social sphere which drew together individuals as well groups, and in trying to understand the pattern of involvement of the rulers in the village as also the nature of alignments within the village, this sphere would seem to be important.

Kalikaṭṭi was not the territorial base of a local chief, nor was it an autonomous, communally-governed *ur*. It was, moreover, the first village of Magare 300. It was, therefore, perhaps inevitable that some administrative arrangement would be made for it from above. A record office, as an inscription of the period of Ballāla II (AD 1209) shows, existed in the village, and major administrative and fiscal decisions pertaining to the village were registered in this office.[38] Inscriptions also refer to at least two generations of *Senabova* officials who were present in the village.[39] But Kalikaṭṭi's seat of administration was not necessarily located in Kalikaṭṭi all the time. *Mahāsāmanta* Siṅgarasa, the first governor of Kalikaṭṭi, was ruling it from Arasikere until he was removed from Arasikere and brought to Kalikaṭṭi.[40] This evidence, apart from showing that Hoysaḷa Viṣṇuvardhana provided 'administration' to Kalikaṭṭi, also perhaps suggests greater measure of calculated action. The grant of authority to rule over Kalikaṭṭi or over an entire *nāḍu* was perhaps of the nature of a service grant. The composition of the subordinate rulers who were granted authority to administer Kalikaṭṭi suggests that they came either from families with local bases or from those which had already attained a high military/administrative rank. The antecedents of *mahāsāmanta* Siṅgarasa, around 1130 and 1132 have already been mentioned. In 1143 *Sāmanta* Goyideva was the ruler of Kalikaṭṭi.[41] Of the various epithets given to Goyideva in the record, one was *Huliyeru-pura-varādhīśvara*. Huliyeru was located in the Karur taluk of Chikmagalur district and was adjacent to Arasikere, and Goyideva was indeed a member of the *Sāmanta* family of Huliyeru-12. In 1139 his eldest brother *Mahāsāmanta* Ceṭṭaya was ruling Huliyeru as a subordinate under Viṣṇuvardhana;[42] in 1148 when *Sāmanta* Goyideva was no longer ruling Kalikaṭṭi, he is found ruling Huliyeru-12 as a *Mahāsāmanta*.[43] Kalikaṭṭi's next ruler Ballanna, mentioned in a record of 1152, rose from the rank of a Perggaḍe or Heggaḍe; he was a *hiriya-heggaḍe* (senior or foremost *Heggaḍe*); he was at the same time *mahāpradhāna senādhipati* and 'a sure arrow in the hands of Viṣṇuvardhana and a *rakṣāpālaka* of Narasiṁha'.[44] *Hiriya-heggaḍe* Ballanna was the ruler of the entire *Magarenāḍu,* and although his background may not have been that of a local ruling family, his military rank and his closeness to two generations of Hoysaḷa rulers are clear enough in the records.

The inscriptions of Kalikaṭṭi next mention three generations of subordinate rulers, all during the reign of Ballāla II. Curiously no antecedents of *mahāsāmanta* Keccanamacaya-*nāyaka*, next ruler of Kalikaṭṭi, are mentioned, although the suffix *nāyaka* in his name seems to correspond to a military rank.[45] His son Ghasane Mahādeva-*nāyaka,* who also ruled Kalikaṭṭi, owed allegiance to *Mahāpradhāna senādhipati hiriya* Bammeya, apparently important warrior during the time of Ballāla II's predecessor Narasiṁha I.[46] *Sāmanta* Ghasane's son *Sāmanta* Someya-*nāyaka* figures in one record at Kalikaṭṭi but it is not clear whether, like his predecessors, he too was ruling Kalikaṭṭi. The record did not originate from him; he is simply praised in it along with various other prominent figures assembled in the village on an occasion when elaborate arrangements were being made to finance the worship of the deity Jagateśvara.[47] In any case, it should be significant that Kalikaṭṭi's inscriptions henceforth seem to cease to refer to the subordinate rulers who had so far been claiming to have been governing it. Before we try to understand if it had any particular significance for Kalikaṭṭi, the impression that *Sāmanta* rule in Kalikaṭṭi declined has to be cross-checked by referring to the history and nature of their involvement in the affairs of the village.

Kalikaṭṭi's inscriptions, because of the nature of their contents, do not associate its rulers with secular acts of administration but show them performing religious acts in the form of installing deities and making grants of land and cash to them. *Mahasāmanta* Siṅgarasa, in keeping with a fairly common practice of early medieval times, installed the deity Siṅgeśvaradeva after his own name in 1130 in a newly created temple and made grants of two types of land in two different parts of the village. The grants, originally made to a Kālāmukha preceptor, were transferred to the *sthānapati* or *sthānika,* the custodian of the temple. Two years later Siṅgarasa associated all the 'subjects' of the village in the act of installing another deity and made similar grants of land. This practice continued through the periods of several other subordinate rulers. When in 1143 brāhmaṇa Āḷvi Bhaṭṭa installed the deity Kaligeśvara, *Sāmanta* Goyideva not only transferred to it five separate plots of land in five different parts of the village, but also imposed levies, both in kind and cash, on oil being produced in the village. Mahāpradhāna Senādhipati Ballanna, although ruling away from the village, made a cash grant and several landgrants to the temple of Jagateśvara which was apparently already in existence.

The reason for cataloguing all these acts is simply that in the absence of any material on how the subordinate rulers were involved in the secular affairs of the village, these acts at least provide an indication as to how they, without a base in the village, were either responding to certain major occasions or were themselves creating such occasions. This pattern seems to have started undergoing a change from the time of *Mahāsāmanta* Keccanamacaya *nāyaka* during the time of Ballāla II. In Keccana's time when the deity Nīleśvaradeva was installed, a temple constructed and a tank excavated, the initiative neither for the construction of the temple nor for the making of land grants came from him. The deity was installed by one Caṭṭabova, a member of the Ekkaṭigar group (i.e. a group consisting of sixty guards), and the landgrants were jointly made by all *Bova-nāyakas, prajā-gāvuṇḍas* and the Jagati *kottali*.[48] Keccana's son Ghasane Mahādeva-*nāyaka,* of course, made a grant of two plots of land to the deity Kammaṭeśvara when it was installed by two individuals Bammoja and Macoja, of the artisan community,[49] but this seems to be the last act of its kind emanating from the subordinate rulers of Kalikaṭṭi.

It seems then that from the early phase of the reign of Ballāla II the role of the subordinate rulers started becoming somewhat insignificant in the internal affairs of Kalikaṭṭi, even if we only take the history of their participation in its religious events as an index of their effective presence in the village. It is not being suggested that prior to the beginning of Ballāla's rule, Kalikaṭṭi's history has to be viewed solely in terms of its subordinate rulers; in fact, its records suggest that Kalikaṭṭi experienced the interplay of other factors simultaneously. What the nature of this interplay was we shall perhaps never fully understand, but we can at least make a beginning by trying to list the various social groups mentioned in the context of Kalikaṭṭi and to understand relationships between these groups.

III

Even this beginning has to be made on the basis of sporadic and incidental references, and a large measure of guesswork will be necessary to see if any connecting thread runs between them. Of particular significance are expressions used in the inscriptions for in most cases, in understanding the status of a social segment or of an individual in a segment, these expressions as well as the order and the context in which they are used seem to provide the only clue.

To digress a little, it has been noted that Kalikaṭṭi was consistently mentioned as a *ur,* once interchangeably with *pattana*[50] and on other occasions with *sthala, nāḍ, agrahāra* and so on. Kalikaṭṭi community's self-identification as a *ur* seems, therefore, to have stretched throughout the major part of the period justifying which inscriptions are available. With its hamlets and perhaps other kinds of extensions, it could be conceived as a *sthala* or a *nāḍ,* more of a locality than a village, but *ur* most probably defined its core settlement and its basic character as a settlement. To define the inhabitants of the *ur,* the term *samastaprajāgalu* has been used several times,[51] but even if it is a general term, it is not certain whether it covered all the categories of village inhabitants. A more specific category was that of *prajā-gāvuṇḍas,* literally, 'subject *gāvuṇḍas*', associated with other groups like the Bovas and the Jagatis on various occasions such as the installation of a deity, grant of consent to donations of land and drafting of documents intended to clarify relations between two groups in the village.[52] The *prajāgāvuṇḍas* were clearly distinct from *prabhu-gāvuṇḍas* and *bhūmiputraka-gāvuṇḍas;* in another contemporary village, Kabballa (Kabala in Kadur tahsil of Chikmagalur district), the *prajā-gāvuṇḍas* are shown as subservient to its *prabhu-gāvuṇḍa* who, in fact, is stated to have been ruling the village under a *mahāsāmanta.*[53] Other groups which were placed above the *prajā-gāvuṇḍas* were the Hoysaḷa-*gāvuṇḍas* and the *Perggaḍes* who too could be heads of villages, either individually or with other members of the family.

Kalikaṭṭi's inscriptions do not refer to *prabhu-gavuṇḍas* or to *perggaḍes,* but in connection with grants of land made to its temples they refer on one occasion to a grant made by a Hoysaḷa-*gāvuṇḍa*[54] and on another to a grant made by a *nāyaka.*[55] They may be considered as important landholders of the village, but not particularly important in the total context of the grants, and they were obviously not rulers of the village.

Among other communities mentioned as inhabiting Kalikaṭṭi was the community of Telligas or oil pressers. An inscription of 1143 lists,[56] among the various donations made to the deity Kaligeśvara, levies on income (*āya*) of the Telligas both in cash and in kind. Of the eight Telligas mentioned in the record, one is called *seṭṭi.* This may imply that the production and the sale of oil (cf. the reference to *haṇa* or coin as annual cash contribution per *gāṇa,* oil-press), were organized by the leader of the community who had the status of a *seṭṭi.* Individual members of the artisan community, some among whom took the initative for installing a deity for the community, also figure as inhabitants of the village.[57]

In Kalikaṭṭi, however, the most significant evidence of participation, both in the major religious acts in the village and in the distribution of its resources, relates to another group called the *Jagati-kottali* or the *Jagati-samūha.* References to them continue to the last record available from Kalikaṭṭi. The occupational particulars of the group are not very clear. They are sometimes described as 'carriers of loads',[58] but this is a vague description and does not somehow seem to be compatible with the eulogistic manner in which they have been mentioned in the records. They are associated with the Jeda-*kottali* (community of weavers) in one record, and in another, when financial arrangements were being made for the worship of the community deity Jagateśvara, the self-imposed contributions on the Jagati-*kottali* were listed under three heads, one head being 'contribution from loom (*maggadere*)'.[59] The community was geographically widespread, as is evident from the expression 'Jagati-*Kotttali* of 7½ lakh country', and Arasikere and Kalikaṭṭi were clearly two important centres associated with their activities.[60]

Inscriptions associated with the *Jagati-kottali* provide some idea of the kind of image which they were trying to project about themselves. They are repeatedly mentioned as excavating tanks, laying out gardens and constructing Śaiva temples: these were all elements constituting an ideal village. But there is more. The greatness of the *Jagati-kottali* was enhanced by the fact that they made, as claimed in a record, Kalikaṭṭi a *pattana,* or a town, and a suitable residence for themselves.[61] It has been noted already that the basic character of Kalikaṭṭi was that of a *ur,* but the *Jagati-kottali* endeavoured to give it the status of a *pattana,* and this endeavour may be seen as a part of their projected self-image, for Kalikaṭṭi did not have the characteristics of a *pattana,* the existence of which in other parts of Karnataka in this period is vouchsafed by inscriptions.[62]

The ascendancy of the Jagati-*kottali* was not an isolated phenomenon for there was another community associated with them in the religious acts, and the acts themselves can be first located in the period when the phase of *Sāmanta* rule in Kalikaṭṭi had started undergoing some change. What it may have meant for Kalikaṭṭi calls for some speculation. A record of 1209, of the time of Ballāla II, contains a curious expression with reference to Mahāpradhāna Kumārapaṇḍitāya Dannāyaka who, according to the expression, was 'a promoter of the crowned consort Umādevī's *kingdom*'.[63] The context seems to suggest that Kalikaṭṭi had by now become a part of the domain over which Umādevī was ruling,[64] and this, apart from explaining the growing insignificance and finally the disappearance of the *Sāmantas,* would also explain the presence of certain social groups and important individuals in the village at this stage.

One group with which the Jagati-*kottali* were associated was that of the Bovas. The Bovas constituted the Ekkaṭigar, the body of sixty 'great' men, sometimes also called *mānasayakkaṭigar.*[65] The Bovas and their Ekkaṭigar group figure in Kalikaṭṭi only from the period of Ballāla II, presumably because the village had come closer to the court by being a part of the domain of the queen, and inscriptions, apart from referring to Bova-*nāyakas* and Ekkaṭigar in general, specifically mention important members of the group like Mārabova, *hiriya* Caṭṭabova (Biṭṭibova), Kalleya, Ketana, Caṭṭabova's son Siṅgabova and others.[66] During the time of *Mahāsāmanta* Keccanamacaya-nāyaka, a deity Nīleśvaradeva was installed by Caṭṭabova in a newly constructed temple; he also constructed a tank. In the landgrants which were made to the temple, the participants were the *prajāgāvuṇḍas,* the *Bova-nāyakas* and the Jagati-*kottali.* Another record, somewhat later in date since it was engraved during the time of *Sāmanta* Someya-*nāyaka,*[67] first refers to the arrangements previously made by Mārabova for the worship of the god Jagatīśvara and then proceeds on to give details of various agrarian and financial arrangements, made with the consent of king Ballāla II, and in the presence of all Jagati-*kottali* of 7½ lakh country, Mārabova, Bāṭṭibova, all *Jagati-kottali* of Kalikaṭṭi, sixty *mānasa-yakkaṭigars* (including Kalleya and Ketana), *Sāmanta* Someya and all the *prajā-gāvuṇḍas* of Kalikaṭṭi (this is the order in which the various participants are mentioned). These two records are important not only because they provide details of what types and amounts of resources were being transferred to the temples but also because they specify the various agencies who either endorsed such transfers or actually parted with their own resources.

Around the same period (between 1208 and 1211), three more records were engraved, one in Kalikaṭṭi and two in Biṭṭena-*halli,* an extension of Kalikaṭṭi which came into existence between 1208 and 1211. They record the religious and other activities of one Hoḍeya Biṭṭeya, son of Mahāpradhāna. Kumārpaṇḍitāya Dannāyaka. Biṭṭeya undertook extension of the village by creating a *halli* in his own same, excavated tanks and installed deities in newly constructed temples. Biṭṭeya was both a recipient of grants and a distributor of them. In 1208,[68] he gave away three separate plots of land to the newly installed deity Somanāthadeva. In 1209,[69] in the presence of all the *prajā-gāvuṇḍas,* the Jagati-*kottali,* the Jeda-*kottali* and the *prajās,* he received a *umbali;* in 1211,[70] he received from the king five *gadyāṇas* (gold coins) in cash and a share in the *modala-siddhāya* (first fixed tax) of Kalikaṭṭi, after having installed the deity Paṇḍiteśvara, named after his father. He invested this cash grant in buying a plot of land for the temple, but the record speaks also of other plots of land which along with the entire Paṇḍiteśvaradevasthāna were made over by Biṭṭeya to Dovayya, obviously the *sthānapati* of Paṇḍiteśvaradevasthāna. Further provisions were made to the effect that two shares would go to Bacarasa and Dyiradeva, individuals presumably associated with the *sthāna.*

Many interconnections embedded in these details are not understandable because the contents of the inscriptions focus brightly on a particular area of activity, leaving other crucial areas in the dark. It is, for example, not possible to reconstruct, from the evidence regarding gifts of land, participation in the gifts and acquisition of new rights in land by recipients of gifts, the totality of the structure of land rights in the village. Donations of land emanated not from one source but a variety of sources; they were endorsed too by various participants. Since the major participants themselves changed from one period to another, it may be guessed that certain rights in the village required to be re-defined from time to time.

Taken together the grants, however, seem to point to one trend: the grants made both in the phase when the *Sāmantas* were active in Kalikaṭṭi and in the subsequent phase when they emanated from different groups and individuals, including the queen, ultimately led to the accumulation of land rights by the temples on a very significant scale.[71] A corresponding development from this must have been an enormous growth of the importance of the *sthānikas* or the heads of the temples, but we can have only an inadequate idea of how much, since between 1215 and 1220 a new phase in the history of Kalikaṭṭi began. It became an *agrahāra.*

IV

Kalikaṭṭi was renamed the immemorial *agrahāra* of Vijaya-Nararasiṁhapura in keeping with the convention of sometimes naming an *agrahāra* or a *maṅgalam* after a king.[72] There is no record to tell us how exactly Kalikaṭṭi became an *agrahāra;*[73] all that is available is that from a certain point of time Kalikaṭṭi was being mentioned in its records as Vijaya-Narasiṁhapura. The conversion of rural settlements into *agrahāras* in the Hoysaḷa kingdom led, in several cases, to flaring up of resistance and violence of an extreme kind,[74] but the passage of Kalikaṭṭi from a *ur* to an *agrahāra* does not seem to have been such a violent transition. It should be a worthwhile exercise to examine to what extent the structure of the *ur* underwent a change as a result of this conversion, but since the material is somewhat inadequate for this phase, only a tenative reconstruction may be offered.

Apparently, the decision to convert Kalikaṭṭi into an *agrahāra* did not change much of its basic character as a rural settlement. In addition to being mentioned as Vijaya-Narasiṁhapura, it continued to be called Kalikaṭṭi *ur;* both names appear together in the inscriptions at this phase.[75] When an agreement was drawn up between the *mahājanas* (i.e. the *brāhmaṇas*) of Vijaya-Narasiṁhapura and its *sthānikas,* it received the consent of the *ur* as well as that of the *Senabova* official located at the village.[76] Two other records from this phase, dated 1227, speak of the creation of *devara-bhāṇḍāras* (cash deposits for the deity), in accordance with *devara-dharma,* for the deities Jagateśvara and Nileśvara, both associated with the Jagati-*kottali.*[77] The composition of the contributors to the *devara-bhāṇḍāra* reveals continued association between the Jagati-*kottali* and the community of Bovas, but there were others too who figure in the list: a *dannāyaka, seṭṭis* and several individuals associated with temples both at and outside Vijaya-Narasiṁhapura (at least one of them in the capacity of a *sthānika*).

Let us, however, take a closer look at the inscriptions of this phase. The documents which speak of the creation of *devara-bhāṇḍāras* for the deities Jagateśvara and Nileśvara emanated from the Jagati-*kottali* of the village; in these documents the Jagati-*kottali* declare themselves unequivocally to be 'worshippers at the feet of the *mahājanas* of Vijaya-Narasiṁhapura'. Here then is an indication of change reflected in the public declaration of allegiance to the brāhmaṇas of the *agrahāra* by a dominant community of Kalikaṭṭi. The declaration of allegiance was a preamble to the recording of a religious act as also of *Jagati-kottali's* association with other groups both inside and outside the village. Was this declaration merely of the nature of a formal acknowledgement of the existence of an *agrahāra* or did it have other implications? In order to answer this question, we start with a significant negative evidence which is that after 1211, some years before we hear of Kalikaṭṭi as an *agrahāra,* no record of Kalikaṭṭi refers to any grant of land made to its temples. In 1227, the Jagati-*kottali* were busy organizing cash deposits for Jagateśvara and Nileśvara according to the *bhāṇḍāra-dharma;* one feels tempted to see in the emergence of the *bhāṇḍāra-dharma* an unavoidable alternative to the series of land donations made to the temples before 1211.

To this nagative evidence may be added details from two records of this period. The first was a *vole* (a written document) given by the *mahājanas* to the *sthānikas* of Kalikaṭṭi,[78] who, under a *sthānapati*, seem to have become a closely knit group by now. The *vole* embodied a direct agreement, endorsed by the *ur* and the *Senabova* official, between the *mahājanas* and the *sthānikas.* It stipulated that of the five *gadyāṇas* (gold coins) which accrued annually to the temples of Kalikaṭṭi and its hamlets, five *haṇas* (equivalent to one-tenth of the amount) would be retained by the *sthānikas* and the rest would go to the *mahājanas.* The agreement, interestingly, is made to look as if it was intended to give certain benefits to the *sthānikas*; what it records, on the other hand, was transfer of cash resources of the temples to the *mahājanas,* only one-tenth of which could now be retained by the *sthānikas.* The agreement incorporated a further provision to the effect that if any additional income emanated from the 'palace', its distribution would be considered in accordance with the custom of the country (*deśamaryāde*).

The document, as mentioned earlier, was endorsed by the *ur.* One could assume, by citing suggestions offered regarding village societies in general,[79] that the *ur* represented a formal body constituted by various segments of the village society, but neither in an earlier phase nor when Kalikaṭṭi became an *agrahāra* did any such formal body exist. What was happening on the other hand was that even in matters like resolving problems of internal adjustment, the social boundaries of the village had to transcend its physical limits. This may perhaps imply that the social organization of the village by itself could not contain all contingent situations. When a second record[80] was drawn up between the *mahājanas* and the *sthānikas,* it was done not merely in the presence of the *prajā* of the village, but in the presence of a great merchant (*Mahāvaḍḍavya-vahāri*), three *prabhu-gāvuṇḍas* of Huliyeru-*nāḍu* and people from four other villages as well. Bearing the signatures of the temple priests, the document was finally endorsed by the same great senior merchant, three *prabhu-gāvuṇḍas* of Huliyeru-*nāḍu,* Binava-*gāvuṇḍa* of Kalikaṭṭi, Bommeya from the 'market', *pattanasvāmī* Lakhi-*seṭṭi* and two temple priests from outside the village. Apparently this kind of representation would ensure conformity to the norm labelled as *deśa-maryāde* in the other record.

The contingent situation which occasioned the document was perhaps the prevailing lack of clarity regarding landrights. The same *sthānikas* who had, in the other record, received the *vole* from the *mahājanas* and who now gave a *vole* to the *mahājanas* 'of their free will' admitted that 'there was much defect in the land of Kammaṭeśvaradeva's *sthāna* ... from the beginning it was not part of the God's endowments. It is not right for the *sthānikas* to dispute about this'. Therefore, 'all lands being enjoyed by us within the lands of all our *sthānas* are ours and lands which the *mahājanas* have been enjoying ever since the *agrahāra* was established are those of the *mahājanas.* So in matters of land either in the main village or in the hamlets, there is no conflict between us and the *mahājanas*'. Not too subtle a denial of a conflict which required representatives from different villages and different segments of rural society to resolve it.

We leave Kalikaṭṭi at this juncture—because there are no more records to take us forward—and we can only wonder as to what the finale was like in the ill-concealed tension between the *mahājanas* and the *sthānikas,* which the conversion of Kalikaṭṭi into an *agrahāra* generated. At the stage in which we leave Kalikaṭṭi it was the *mahājanas* who clearly held the advantage, but it would perhaps be wrong to assume that to be the final word about this village. After all, the position Kalikaṭṭi was to occupy in relation to the prevalent political organization was defined time and again by rulers whose control extended to it; it is unlikely that the process would have stopped after the *mahājanas* took over.

NOTES

1. The texts and translations of these inscriptions are available in B. Lewis Rice, ed., *Epigraphia Carnatica* (hereafter *EC*), vol. 5, Mangalore, 1902.
2. This identification was also suggested by M.H. Krishna, *EC,* vol. 15, *Supplementary Inscriptions in the Hassan District,* Mysore, 1943, AK 215. For the location of Kanakatte, a circle headquarter, in the northern tip of Arasikere taluk, between Chikmagalur District in the west and Tumkur District in the east, see the map in *Mysore State Gazetteer: Hassan District,* Bangalore, 1971.
3. For the history of the Hoysaḷas see J.D.M. Derrett, *The Hoysaḷas: A Medieval Indian Royal Family*, Oxford University Press, 1957.
4. M.H. Krishna, *EC,* vol. 15, AK 215,
5. *EC,* 5, AK 41.

6. G.S. Dikshit, *Local Self-Government in Medieval Karnataka,* Dharwar, 1964, Chapter I.
7. *EC*, 5, AK 41.
8. For the network of Kālāmukha sect and centres in Karnataka see David Lorenzen, *The Kapalikas and Kalamukhas,* Delhi, 1972, Chapter 5; R.N. Nandi, *Religious Institutions and Cults in the Deccan, c.AD* 600-*AD* 1000, Delhi, 1973, pp. 85-90; also his, 'Origin and Nature of Saivite Monasticism: The case of Kalamukhas', in *Indian Society: Historical Probings*, eds. R.S. Sharma and V. Jha, Delhi, 1974, pp. 190-201.
9. For Noḷambabāḍi 32,000 and Ucchaṅgi, the centre of Noḷamba power to the south of the Tungabhadra, see J.D.M. Derrett, *The Hoysaḷas,* p. 12 and map on p. 5.
10. *EC,* 5, AK 45.
11. Ibid., AK 48.
12. Ibid.
13. See Introduction of this Volume.
14. See *EC* (revd. edn.), vol. 5 (Mysore District), Mysore, 1976, pp. 692, 714, 850 etc.
15. R.P. Kulkarni, 'Irrigation Engineering in India', *Indian Journal of History of Sciences,* vol. 17, no. 1, 1982.
16. See Appendix 2 of this volume.
17. For construction of sluices in south India, which may have been similar to those in the Deccan, see Rajan Gurukkal, 'Aspects of the Reservoir System of Irrigation in the early Pandya State', *Studies in History,* new series, vol. 2, no. 2, 1986, pp. 155-64.
18. The gift in this case was of 300 *kammas* of dry land, *EC,* 5, AK 42.
19. Ibid., AK 55.
20. See Appendix 3 of this volume.
21. See Appendix 2 of this volume.
22. *EC,* 5, AK 55.
23. Ibid.
24. Ibid.
25. Ibid., AK 45.
26. Ibid., AK 40; EC, 6, KA 117, KA 118.
27. *EC,* 5, AK 40.
28. Ibid., AK 55.
29. Ibid., AK 46.
30. Ibid., AK 52.
31. Ibid., AK 46.
32. Ibid., AK 51; *EC*, 6, KA 117.
33. *EC,* 5, AK 40.
34. Ibid., 5, AK 51.
35. Ibid., 6, KA 117, KA 118.
36. Ibid., 5, AK 40.
37. The gift was of 75 *Kambas* of garden land under the big tank, *EC,* 6, AK 40.

38. *EC,* 5, AK 40.
39. Ibid.; also AK 51.
40. Ibid., 5, AK 41, AK 45.
41. Ibid., 5, AK 55.
42. Ibid., 6, Kd 32.
43. Ibid., Kd 34.
44. Ibid., 5, AK 52.
45. Ibid., AK 46.
46. Ibid., AK 42.
47. Ibid., AK 48.
48. Ibid., AK 46.
49. Ibid., AK 42.
50. Ibid., AK 48.
51. For example, Ibid., AK 45.
52. Inscription of the time of Ballāla II, ibid., AK 48.
53. *EC,* 6, Kd 32, Kd 34; see also Ibid., Kd 69. These records show that it is totally inadequate to translate the term *gāvuṇḍa* as 'village headman'. *Gāvuṇḍa* in general stands for cultivator and the actual status of an individual cultivator may be determined by taking note of such prefixes as *prajā, prabhu, bhūmiputraka, Hoysaḷa,* etc.
54. *EC,* 5, AK 55.
55. Ibid.
56. Ibid.
57. Ibid., AK 42.
58. This is one of the meanings suggested in F. Kittel, *A Kannada-English Dictionary,* Delhi, repr., 1983, p. 629.
59. *EC, 5,* AK 48.
60. Ibid. While the inscriptions do not suggest what the nature of the group was, the various expressions used in relation to the *Jagati* point to the existence of a group. The expressions are *samasta-Jagatīya-Kottali, Jagatīya-Kottali, Jagati-Samūham,* etc. (EC, 5, AK 40, 46, 47, 48). The association of the Jagatis with well-known merchant groups such as the Ayyavole and the *Mummuridaṇḍam* suggests that they too constituted a merchant group of considerable local importance; G.S. Dikshit, *Local Self-Government in Medieval Karnataka,* p. 147. The Jagatis carried or transported loads (as merchants), paid loom-tax, in addition to contribution to, Jagatīśvara, worshipped Nīleśvara (the deity of the dye?) and were associated with the *Jeda-Kottali* or the community of weavers. There is thus a strong possibility that the Jagati organization not only dealt in textile merchandise but were also closely involved in its production. For reference to Jedas or the caste of weavers see Vijaya Ramaswamy, *Textiles and Weavers in Medieval South India*, 1985, p. 14.
61. *EC,* 5, AK 48.
62. B.D. Chattopadhyaya, 'Urban centres in early medieval India: an overview', in *The Making of Early Medieval India*; also G.S. Dikshit, *Local Self-Government,* Chapters 7 and 8.

63. *EC,* 5, AK 40.
64. Umādevī was the second queen of Ballāla II. See Derrett, *The Hoysaḷas,* p. 204.
65. See, for Garuḍas, Sivanna's book on Hoysaḷa polity. As in the case of the *Jagati-Kottali,* in Ekkaṭigar's case too, it would be difficult to offer a satisfactory explanation regarding the nature of the organization. *Ekkaṭiga* means 'great man' or 'strong man' and from the contexts in which the term *Ekkaṭigar* occurs, it would appear that they were a group of armed retainers of the members of the royalty and of other rulers like *Mahāmaṇḍaleśvaras.* In Kalikaṭṭi, the presence of the *Ekkaṭigar* from the period when it passed under the direct control of the Hoysaḷas during Ballāla II'*s* reign, therefore, seems significant. An inscription, dated 1095, from Yedur in the Somaverpet taluk of Coorg district, refers to 250 *Ekkaṭigaru* along with other groups who are said to have been under departed *Mahāmaṇḍaleśvara* Duddarasa's command (*EC,* vol. I, revd. edn., Mysore, 1972, no. 62). This confirms the possibility of their serving as a group of armed retainers. For parallel institutions in other parts of south India see two papers by M.G.S. Narayanan, 'The institution of Companions of honour with special reference to south India', *Journal of Indian History* (Golden Jubilee Number, 1973), pp. 181-92 and 'The hundred groups and the rise of Nayar militia in Kerala', *Proceedings of the Indian History Congress,* 1983, p. 113 ff.

    There are suggestions in the Kalikaṭṭi records that the *Ekkaṭigar* was constituted by the community of Bovas; the prominent members of the *Ekkaṭigar,* participating in religious acts at the village, had *bova* suffixed to their names. Elsewhere too, *bova* figured as a suffix to proper names of archers who constituted themselves into a group, called *Billa munurvvaru* or 'three hundred men of the bow' and are found offering protection to mercantile groups (*South Indian Inscriptions,* vol. 15, pp, 46, 253). A search for the Bovas who obviously formed several types of mercenary groups may lead one to the Bedas, Bedars or Boyas, the Boyis of Telengana and Ramoshis of Marathawada. The Bedas were extensively distributed in south Karnataka, and the segments of hunters and agriculturists correspond respectively to the Ur Bedas and Myasa Bedas. The segment variously known as 'children of chiefs', 'king's children', 'Valmika ksatriyas' derived legitimacy by serving in army, and the mercenary tradition among the Bedas may be traced back to periods of Vijayanagar, and Hyder Ali and Tipu Sultan. For Bedas see H.V. Nanjundayya, *Beda Caste* (No. 3 in The *Ethnographical Survey of Mysore,* Bangalore, 1906); H.V. Nanjundayya and L.K. Ananthakrishna Iyer, *The Mysore Tribes and Castes,* vol. 2 (Mysore University, 1928); also 'Bedar or Boya' in E. Thurston and K. Rangachari, *Castes and Tribes of Southern India,* vol. I, Madras, 1909, pp. 180-209.
66. *EC,* 5 AK 46.
67. Ibid., AK 48.
68. Ibid., 6, KA 117.
69. Ibid., 5, AK 40.

70. Ibid., 6, KA 118.
71. See Appendix 3 of this Volume.
72. For a list of such settlements in the Coḷa country see Y. Subbarayalu, *Political Geography of the Chola Country*, which gives lists of villages under *nāḍus*.
73. No formal order from the king converting Kalikaṭṭi *ur* into an *agrahāra* is incorporated in any of its records. Only, from a point of time onward the records start referring to it as 'immemorial *agrahāra* Vijaya-Narasiṁhapura'. Perhaps the earliest record referring to Kalikaṭṭi as an *agrahāra* dates to around 1215; *EC,* 5, AK 51.
74. See Introduction, note 29; also J.D.M. Derrett, *The Hoyasaḷas,* p. 181.
75. EC, 5, AK 47, AK 50, AK 51.
76. Ibid., AK 49, AK 51.
77. Ibid., AK 47, AK 50.
78. Ibid., AK 51.
79. Works on early medieval Karnataka discuss functioning of the village assembly, although it is not clear from such works what the structure of the *ur,* considered in terms of such functioning, would have been like. See G.S. Dikshit, *Local Self-Government in Medieval Karnataka,* Chapter 3; A.V. Venkataratnam, 'Village autonomy under the Hoysalas', in *The Hoysala Dynasty*, ed. B. Sheikh Ali, 1972, pp. 137-40.
80. *EC,* 5, AK 49.

Appendix 1

Sāmantas of Kalikaṭṭi

Date	*Hoysaḷa King*	*Name and title of Sāmanta*	*Reference*
1130	Viṣṇuvardhana	*Mahasāmanta* Siṅgarasa of Arasikere	*EC*, 5, AK 41
1132	Viṣṇuvardhana	*Mahasāmanta* Siṅgarasa of Kalikaṭṭi	*EC*, 5, AK 45
1143	Narasiṁha I	*Sāmanta* Goyideva	*EC*, 5, AK 55
1152	Narasiṁha I	*Mahapradhāna* Senādhipati *hiriya heggaḍe* Ballanna	*EC*, 5, AK 52
?	Ballāla II	*Mahasāmanta* Keccanamacaya-*nāyaka*	*EC*, 5, AK 46
?	Ballāla II	*Sāmanta* Ghasanemahādeva-nāyaka, son of *Mahasāmanta* Keccanamacaya-*nāyaka* (he was subordinate to *mahāpradhāna* senādhipati *hiriya* Bammeya who in turn had been subordinate to Narasiṁha)	*EC*, 5, AK 42
1189	Ballāla II	*Sāmanta* Someyanāyaka, son of Ghasanemahādeva-*nāyaka* (it is not certain that he was actually a ruler of the village)	*EC*, 5, AK 48

Inscriptions dated after 1189 do not refer to rule by a *Sāmanta*

Appendix 2

Tanks and Other Sources of Water at Kalikaṭṭi

	Dates	*Frequency of Reference*	*Reference*
1. *Hiriya-kere* (big tank)	1130	1	*EC*, 5, AK 41
	1132	1	*EC*, 5, AK 45
	1143	1	*EC*, 5, AK 55
	1152	1	*EC*, 5, AK 52
	—	1	*EC*, 5, AK 42
	1189	2	*EC*, 5, AK 48
	1211	1	*EC*, 6, KA 118
2. *Āḍuva-gere*	1143	3	*EC*, 5, AK 55
3. Hariyoja's tank	1132	1	*EC*, 5, AK 45
4. *Niru-gaṭṭa* (*Kere*)	1152	1	*EC*, 5, AK 52
	—	1	*EC*, 5, AK 46
	1189	1	*EC*, 5, AK 48
5. *Halla* (stream)	—	1	*EC*, 5, AK 46
6. *Bayikalu* (channel)	1143	1	*EC*, 5, AK 55
7. *Kanne-gere* (virgin tank or newly constructed tank)	1209	1	*EC*, 5, AK 40
8. Boviti's tank	1209	1	*EC*, 5, AK 40
9. *Biṭṭeya samudra*	1209	2	*EC*, 5, AK 40
10. Maṅgeya's tank	1208	1	*EC*, 6, KA 117
	1209	1	*EC*, 5, AK 40
	1211	1	*EC*, 6, KA 118

* Kalikaṭṭi inscription of 1189 refers to two other tanks close to which plots of wet land were granted: (1) Mahādeva's tank in Banni-*kere* and (2) big tank at Niḍu-*valli*, *EC*, 5, AK 48. It is not, however, certain whether they were located in Kalikaṭṭi.

Appendix 3

Temples, Priests and Patrons at Kalikaṭṭi

Deity/Temple		*Priests*/Sthānikas *associated with*	*Deity installed by*	*Donor*	*Nature of grant*	*Reference*
1. Siṅgeśvaradeva	1130	(i) Kālāmukha Kriyāśakti-paṇḍita, disciple of *Naiṣṭhikamaṭha-ācārya* Pareśvara-paṇḍita (ii) Rāmadeva, son of the *sthānapati* of Siṅgeśvara	*Mahasāmanta* Siṅgarasa	Siṅgarasa	(i) wet land (ii) dry land	*EC*, 5, AK 41
2. Beṭṭada-Kalideva	1132	(i) Śaiva priest Śekara-Jiya, grandson of Beṭṭada-Jiya	*Mahasāmanta* Siṅgarasa	Siṅgarasa	(i) wet land (ii) two plots of dry land	*EC*, 5, AK 45
3. Kaligeśvara	1143	Āḷvi-Bhaṭṭa	Āḷvi-Bhaṭṭa	(i) *Sāmanta* Goyideva (ii) Sataya-*nāyaka*, grandson of Hoysaḷa-*gāvuṇḍa*	(i) Five separate plots of land (ii) measure of oil (iii) 1 *haṇa* (cash) per *ghāṇa* (oil mill)	*EC*, 5, AK 55

(*contd.*)

(*Contd.*)

Deity/Temple		*Priests/*Sthānikas *associated with*	*Deity installed by*	*Donor*	*Nature of grant*	*Reference*
4. Jagateśvara or Jagatīśvara	1152	Śivaśakti-paṇḍita, *sthānapati* of Jagateśvara		(iii) Telligas Mahapradhāna Senādhipati Ballanna	(i) 3 separate plots of land (ii) Dry land (iii) Cash (*Gadyāṇa*)	EC, 5, AK 52
	1189	Kālāmukha Kalyāṇa-śakti-paṇḍita, disciple of Śiva-śakti-paṇḍita, disciple of Nāga-śakti-paṇḍita		Associated with the grants were: (i) Jagati-*kottali* of 7½ country (ii) Jagatis of Kalikaṭṭi (iii) 60 manasa-yakkaṭigar (iv) individual Bovas, (v) *prajāgāvuṇḍas* of Kalikaṭṭi (vi) *Sāmanta* Someya-*nāyaka*	(i) 6 separate plots of land (ii) marriage tax of *hana* (iii) 3 separate contributions from Jagati-*kottali*	*EC*, 5, AK 51

(*contd.*)

(*Contd.*)

Deity/Temple		*Priests*/Sthānikas *associated with*	*Deity installed by*	*Donor*	*Nature of grant*	*Reference*
	1215	Jagati-Jiya (several other *Jiyas* or Śaiva priests mentioned, but it is not clear whether they too were associated with the Jagatīśvara temple)				*EC*, 5, AK 51
	1227	Rājaguru, *sthānika* of Jagatīśvara		31 persons making grants, all grants apparently being in cash		*EC*, 5 AK 50
5. Nileśvaradeva	—	Lākula Śaiva Kumāra Siṅgi-paṇḍita	Caṭṭabova	(i) *Boya-nāyakas*, *prajāgāvuṇḍas* and Jagati-*kottali* (ii) Queen Umādevī	Two separate plots of wet land	*EC*, 5, AK 46
	1227	—	—	Grants made by Jagatis and Bovas		*EC*, 5, AK 47
6. Kammaṭeśvara	—	—	Bammoja and Macoja	*Sāmanta* Ghasane-mahādeva-*nāyaka*	2 separate plots of land	*EC*, 5, AK 52

(*contd.*)

(*Contd.*)

Deity/Temple		*Priests*/Sthānikas *associated with*	*Deity installed by*	*Donor*	*Nature of grant*	*Reference*
	1215	Jiyas	—		—	*EC*, 5, AK 49
7. Mūlasthāna-Kalideva	1209	*Sthānapati Sena-bova* Madayya				*EC*, 5, AK 40
8. Somanātha-deva	1208	Chikajiya	Hoḍeya Biṭṭeya	Hoḍeya Biṭṭeya	3 separate plots of land	*EC*, 6, KA 117
9. Paṇḍiteśvara-deva	1211	Dovayya, Bacarasa and Dyiradeva	Hoḍeya Biṭṭeya	Hoḍeya Biṭṭeya	3 separate plots of land	*EC*, 6, KA 118

Five

Conclusion

Conceptual and historiographical stereotypes regarding India's villages have had a long standing, and despite the impressive turnout of monographs and fruitful theoretical exercises in recent years,[1] the stereotypes continue to figure powerfully in some brands of historical writings. The stereotypes have in fact often been used to reinforce attempts to work out processes of change in Indian history, although the stereotypes themselves project the image of a rural world which hardly underwent any change. The empirical data presented earlier were not collated with the primary intention of urging a restructuring of the historians' ways of thinking about villages and village societies of the past; the effort essentially constituted a plea to the undertaking of research, as yet very much inadequate, on rural society in different periods of Indian history. Nevertheless, we believe that the data, selected from documents, spanning almost a millennium of Indian history, do entitle us at least to suggest a few points relating to how rural settlements and rural societies of the past may be viewed.

The initial point relates to the unit of study. Viewing rural settlements and, by implication, village communities as isolates does not, for one thing, take cognizance of settlement hierarchies, and such hierarchies, it needs to be stressed, do not necessarily imply distinction between urban and rural settlements alone. Hierarchies could exist in rural space, and since settlement size is not always a satisfactory determinant of hierarchy, the concept of hierarchy can be considered in terms of both how rural residents were socially organized and how differentially individual villages existed in rural landscape. Rural space did not consist of single units in a vacuum; nor did it extend to horizontal infinity. There may have been different levels at which individual units, with variations within them, could intersect. Viewing rural settlements not simply as undifferentiated landmass would lead to acknowledging the possibility of the existence of nodes even in rural space and of change.

Change, of course, would relate to historical processes which could originate at the rural level or elsewhere.

Differentiation among rural settlements and the historical reality of village units coming together are attested by the inscriptions of Bengal and Karnataka analysed above. What distinguished one village from another is not clear; the inscriptions do not provide any idea regarding the sizes of rural settlements and very little regarding the size and composition of rural population. Nevertheless, Kalikaṭṭi was a 'foremost village'; in Gupta and post-Gupta Bengal too several villages could be considered as of greater importance than others. However, Kalikaṭṭi was not, even when it was an *agrahāra,* self-contained. There could be situations where issues arising out of the village could be resolved in accordance with what a Kalikaṭṭi inscription terms as *deśa-maryādā. Deśa-maryādā* which can only loosely be translated as 'practice of the land' does not refer to the whole country; it perhaps points to a social sphere which transcended even the foremost village. It did not have to be a formally constituted sphere. It could be an abstraction of a practice, very much like the practice in contexts in which landsale transactions were taking place in Gupta and post-Gupta Bengal and which would draw select representatives from different settlements together when the need arose. The inter-village networks then do not have to be viewed from the point of view of familial or caste ties alone. There could be other forms of linkages of varying length, but since the accent of these essays has been, because of the nature of the source material, on things political, a few clarifications regarding that aspect may be in order.

If we can leave aside such facile notions as villages in the past existing as little republics or as settlement units the state merely drew revenue from, then a major point that can be raised is: how does rural society figure in the political processes in different phases of Indian history? In answering this, one would have to go beyond ascertaining whether the monarch was more active in performing his duties towards the village than he is generally supposed to have been.[2] The query itself implies that at different points of time in history, rural society may have undergone different experiences and that these experiences were generated by changes far wider than the attitude of a passive/active or benevolent/despotic monarch.

For the early medieval period, it is often argued that landgrants hold the key to understanding the historical processes in operation. Since the landgrants constitute the major source, the brāhmaṇas, either as individuals or as groups or in association with religious centres, are seen as key actors in the context of various processes such as agrarian expansion in the wake of urban decay, emergence of rural stratification, crystallization of landed estates and so on. Agrarian expansion, implying proliferation of rural settlements, could be a regular, continuing process in pre-modern times, but systematic documentation corroborating this trend for different regional contexts in the early medieval period is still rather meagre. Also implicit is the role assigned to the brāhmaṇas in the process of agrarian expansion, by underlining the rights bestowed on them, is the assumption that cleavage in rural society, with two opposite points in the pole, was largely brought about by the practice of landgrants. The manner of reference to the brāhmaṇas in Gupta period inscriptions hardly warrants a sharp differentiation between the brāhmaṇas and other residents of a village. At a much later date, at Kalikaṭṭi too, the brāhmaṇas do not at all figure prominently before its conversion as an *agrahāra.* The case study on rural settlements in the domain of the Nadol Cāhamānas further points to the nature of complexity which a study of the emergence of rural settlements and of their structure in an initially marginal area is likely to reveal. In any case, irrespective of whether a region is considered nuclear or marginal, the complexity in either context can hardly be grasped by making a single social group spearhead the process of change.

Perhaps a concept like that of the 'dominant caste' which is found to be relevant in discussing contemporary rural India could have offered an alternative perspective if its application to earlier times could be tested with empirical evidence. Nevertheless, early medieval documents do offer alternatives to the somewhat simplistic picture of brāhmaṇa-dominated rural society, or, at the most, of a society polarized between the local lords, the *bhogikas,* the *ṭhakkuras* and an undifferentiated mass of common residents. The Gupta inscriptions already show us that the important segments of the rural society were the *kuṭumbins* and the *mahattaras* who could be distinguished from other residents and that with the passage of time further hierarchical groupings of non-brāhmaṇa rural residents are suggested by such categories as *mahāmahattara* and *mahāpradhāna.* In south Karnataka too a somewhat similar pattern is suggested by the distinction among different *gāvuṇḍa* groups, by the presence of the *nāyakas* and of other categories, including the *sāmantas,* which would make the structure of its village society much more complex than simple polarization. What needs to be noted in particular is that the process of the emergence of these categories does not precede the rise in status of the brāhmaṇas as recipients of land or the proliferation of brāhmaṇa dominated rural settlements; both are simultaneous processes. Both would bear upon the study of the complexity of rural stratification in early medieval India.

Admittedly, the processes themselves had regional variations, and it is, thus, necessary to comprehend in detail the structure of rural society in its varied regional contexts in order to be able to analyse its relationship with the state. Let us make it clear at this stage that we do not consider that rural settlements in a *janapada* stand at a distance, as separate entities, from the state, but are integral components of the totality of the state structure. At the same time, there may be reorientations of the relationship between the different components, for example, the apex power represented by a ruling lineage and the rural settlements. Reorientatien, by and large, may be viewed as a historical process, in which both the structure of the rural society at a regional level (and not simply individual villages) and the structure of the apex undergo change, the nature of change deriving from—and at the same time bearing upon—the nature of their mutual relationship. The shift to regional power centres from the expansive Gupta empire in post-Gupta Bengal coincided with some very crucial changes in the rural society in the form of the proliferation of *agrahāra* settlements, emergence of new categories of important landholders and elaboration of the local-level administrative apparatus, in which prominent local residents may be assumed to have been inducted. The crystallization of the regional state from the early Pāla period onward seems to have brought the apex of the structure into direct relationship through its administrative apparatus, with its rural bases. This not only obliterated the levels at which rural residents could make their presence felt but also possibly, and without design, created areas of tension between the apex power and those elements in rural society which had, in previous times, occasionally acted as a cohesive group in local administration.

The different stages of the history of Kalikaṭṭi too reveal different patterns of relationship with the apex power. While certain general changes took place at the level of the rural society itself (and these general changes would be comparable to changes elsewhere), the specific changes at Kalikaṭṭi culminating, in our period, in its conversion into an *agrahāra,* derived from its linkage with the apex power, the Hoyasaḷas. In the pre-Hoysaḷa period too, its status had changed from a non-descript rural settlement to a *vṛtti.* In the Hoysaḷa period, the inscriptions suggest at least three different phases in which the apex power reoriented its relationship with the village. In the Nadol

Cāhamāna kingdom in western Rajasthān the pattern of reorientation derived essentially from the structure of the apex power itself; the essence of this reorientation was the way assignments were made, requiring frequent realignments of individual villages.

In underlining the essential integrality of rural society with the State, it is not being suggested that villages were no more than 'architectural and demographic entities';[3] the ways in which individual villages figure as specific reference points in epigraphy, literature and other sources—as also in the life experiences of village residents—would negate such a viewpoint. The unique profile of an individual village, thus, certainly merits one kind of academic enquiry. At the same time, since this profile could undergo changes in numerous ways—through the expansion of a village or its desertion, its conversion into an *agrahāra* settlement or its emergence as a nodal point in rural space—another kind of enquiry will have to undertake analyses of the historical contexts in which individual villages existed. Villages, in interaction with one another both spatially and socially, constituted entities above the village, which could further interlock, and one often finds such entities drawing representatives of village residents together. Villages, apart from being resource bases of the State, could thus indicate the points of communication across space and the nature of stratification which was the foundation of the state structure. How the apex power reached across to the distribution of power in rural society—whether down to the level of individual villages or to the supra-village entities, whether through adjustments or through exercise of greater control—is a theme which will require probing into both the structure of apex power and the structure of rural society in different periods of history. This cannot be done by keeping village studies permanently relegated to the ahistorical framework of traditional India.

NOTES

1. For a review of social anthropological literature on Indian villages and of relevant issues see M.N. Srinivas, 'The Indian Village: Myth and Reality', in *The Dominant Caste and Other Essays*, Delhi, 1987, pp. 20–59.
2. Srinivas, 'The Indian Village'.
3. L. Dumont, op. cit.; also L. Dumont and D. Pocock, 'Village Studies', *Contributions to Indian Sociology*, no. 1, 1957, pp. 23–42.

Index